X's and O's *Don't Mean* I Love You

THE UNTOLD STORY OF THE NFL'S FIRST FEMALE SCOUT

As told by Connie Nicholas Carberg
with Elisabeth Meinecke

St. Jude Press

Elisabeth Meinecke/St. Jude Press
Troy, MO
www.ConnieScouts.com

Book Layout ©2013 BookDesignTemplates.com
Cover design by Jenna Carberg

Ordering Information:
Quantity sales. Special discounts are available on quantity purchases by corporations, associations, and others. For details, contact the "Special Sales Department" at the address above.

X's and O's Don't Mean I Love You/ Elisabeth Meinecke.
—1st ed.
ISBN 978-0-692-67437-6

Contents

Part III: Validation

To four people without whom this book would not have been possible:

Dr. Calvin and Evelyn Nicholas

David and Dianna Meinecke

" ... It was the watershed moment every sports hero faces, the process by which sports history self-selects. The quarterback, picking the turf out of his helmet; the boxer, bruised and spent with blood streaming down his face; the pitcher, staring down the batter with the bases loaded in the ninth—all must face the challenge of response in adversity's wake. The results separate the legends from those forgotten in the passing of generations: the great ones get back up, fight, and become stronger. Those who fade away, who let defeat become discouragement—they are the names never remembered, except in cautionary tales. ... "

To Whom It May Concern:

The primary purpose of this letter is to tell you that Connie ... is an outstanding young lady who accomplishes unbelievable things.

— LOU HOLTZ
UNIVERSITY OF NOTRE DAME
1995

PROLOGUE

It was 1977, and the sports world was moving backwards.

Only a year before, supported by team coaches and scouts, Jets general manager Al Ward had made a gutsy, historic call: he'd given a young employee named Connie Nicholas scouting responsibilities along with her secretarial work. The move was unprecedented—a female scout had never been tried before in the NFL, where a woman working in a football office generally meant one of two things: she took notes and answered phones, or she owned part of the franchise, neither of which demanded the intimate, day-to-day knowledge of football that scouting required. There was little public relations benefit in the mid-1970s for such an avant-garde decision, but Ward, impressed by the young woman's football savvy, recognized her scouting potential and decided she should have the chance to fulfill it. Later, he informed the Jets owners of his decision, which they accepted with minimal questions.

But now, change was coming. Thin, wispy Leon Hess, an oil tycoon who had once served as an Army officer fueling Gen. Patton's tanks during World War II, was one of a handful of people who had purchased the Jets back in 1963 for $1 million. In 1977, for the first time, he became acting president of the club, then in a general state of turnover. They'd been through four head coaches in two seasons and were losing their franchise quarterback, Joe Namath, to aging knees. But Hess had experience wresting success from adversity—he'd turned a single oil delivery truck acquired during the Great Depression into a petroleum empire. When it came to the Jets, he wasn't afraid to do things his way. He had several changes he wanted made—one of which directly involved Connie. Ward had tried dissuading him, but Hess remained firm, leaving his general manager with the thankless task of informing his young employee. Ward knew the news would almost break her heart.

Reluctantly, he broached the topic with Connie, a tall, vivacious young woman in her mid-20s, who worked such long days it seemed she'd never learned what office hours were. Nothing in her brief career could have readied her for what was coming. Her football knowledge was irreproachable; even the head coach, Walt Michaels, who had talked football with her since she was 12, valued her opinion. People found her passion for the franchise infectious. She dressed in prisms of Jets green and white, was optimistic even when they lost (which they did frequently), and was always helping fans meet players or secure autographs. Once, not long ago, she'd rung up a young neighborhood boy and informed him Joe Namath was coming to her family's house for a physical, since her father was one of the Jets' doctors and his office was located at the Nicholas home. The boy dashed over on his bike; he and a group of about five other autograph hopefuls lined up on the Nicholas couch and waited. When Joe appeared, he signed for all of them. The boy even managed to grab the Coke can the quarterback left behind as a treasured memento. Such anecdotes were common among the young woman's acquaintances. Others may have been the face of the franchise; she was its heart.

She was listening now as Ward dispatched his awkward errand: Mr. Hess, it seemed, was uncomfortable with a woman representing the team on scouting trips, essentially serving as a spokesperson for the Jets to major colleges and at big-time Bowl events. Traveling was like oxygen to scouts; they visited schools and marquee games to get an in-person look at players and glean valuable information about their personalities and family history. Except for Connie, a woman doing such things was generally unheard of, an uncomfortable divergence from how most NFL teams presented themselves. From now on, Hess had decided, Connie could still perform some scouting responsibilities, but she would be bound to roles within Jets facilities. Her other duties would remain—secretarial support to the scouting department, grading film the Jets had acquired, helping prepare for the draft—but she could no longer travel for the team in a scouting capacity for one reason: she was a woman.

It was the watershed moment every sports hero faces, the process by which sports history self-selects. The quarterback, picking the turf out of his helmet; the boxer, bruised and spent with blood streaming down his face; the pitcher, staring down the batter with the bases loaded in the ninth—all must face the challenge of response in adversity's wake. The results separate the legends from those forgotten in the passing of generations: the great ones get back up, fight, and become stronger. Those who fade away, who let defeat become discouragement—they are the names never remembered, except in cautionary tales.

Steeled by natural gumption and the sports environment that had nurtured her, Connie fought back.

True to herself, it wasn't in a conventional sense. Confronting Leon Hess, filing a lawsuit, or stirring up trouble in the press never occurred to her. Her work had never been about making a statement. It had been about following her passion. And a female scouting in the NFL was so novel, so unconventional, so unlike anything the league had witnessed prior to her that even she had yet to fully appreciate the magnitude of her achievement.[i] How could she fault Leon Hess for doing the same?

And so she conveyed to Al Ward that she understood. She was poised to do whatever Jets management felt was in the team's best interest. She was "Connie from the Jets," and she still loved them.

Then she went out and helped scout one of the best players the organization ever drafted.

Coming out of college in 1979, this young defensive end had eye-popping speed and, as one NFL coach later described, "the heart of an Arabian horse." But there were red flags, too—like when he left an illustrious football powerhouse early in his career to play for a small, out-of-the-way school in Oklahoma, where the players' equipment looked like cast-offs and reeked of mildew. As time expired on his final collegiate season at the end of '78, pro football hesitated, and the young man waited, in danger of being forgotten, until Connie, scouring through scouting reports and film archives that winter, came across his file. As she picked up the phone to call a list of prospects, she had no idea she was about to make the biggest discovery of her career—a unheralded but talented misfit who would storm into NFL record books and join only sixteen other men, out of the countless players in franchise history, in the team's prestigious Ring of Honor. But first, it would take a woman's eye to spot what everyone else had missed.

The moment was almost twenty years in the making.

Part I: The Foundation

I have observed [Connie] through junior and senior high school—always pleasant, always ready to learn, forever helpful.

— WALT MICHAELS
FORMER HEAD COACH
NEW YORK JETS

CHAPTER 1

The Game Begins

The winds blew playfully through much of that New York September, as if debating whether to chase away summer. But by month's end, cooling temperatures reassured a teeming city that football season had begun.

Connie Nicholas was 11 years old when, in the fall of 1962, her father began working as a sideline physician at professional football games. The team, then called the New York Titans, later the New York Jets, was a fledgling franchise of the American Football League (AFL), founded in 1959 as a rival to the older, more powerful National Football League (NFL). They played in a doomed stadium known as the Polo Grounds, soon to be sacrificed for a Manhattan housing project. Once, it had produced legends—an over-the-shoulder catch by Willie Mays, so jaw-dropping that it was simply called "The Catch"; a glorious ninth-inning swing of the bat by Bobby Thomson, which wrested a pennant from his team's crosstown foes and set even the press box screaming.[i] But by twilight of '63, the stadium's turf had fallen into neglect, so much so that, two days before a football game in late November, a groundhog's hole went unfixed on the field, which a wide receiver, practicing a route, stepped in and sprained his ankle. On leaving the field to ice it, he heard a shocking announcement over the radio: President John F. Kennedy had just been assassinated in Dallas. As his teammates came off the field, he broke the horrific news. That day, a pall shrouded the stadium.

In general, the scene that greeted fans of the team in those early years as they traipsed toward the Polo Grounds was one of only tenuous optimism. They witnessed a team that, while talented, lost as frequently as it won, failed to sign a single pick from the 1963 draft, and, for the first two seasons of its existence, didn't even have playbooks. That season, the average player salary in the prestigious NFL was $20,000, which was just over three times the national average, yet miniscule compared to the luxury their successors would enjoy. Throughout the decade, plenty of players worked in the off-season; you might find your local football star selling insurance during the summer months.[ii] Connie's father, Dr. Calvin Nicholas, would spend his first few seasons on the team's medical staff with no compensation. From the dilapidated venue to the uneven play, there wasn't much for the sparse crowd to cheer.

Yet Connie was riveted. As she watched from the stands during the early '60s, the action before her felt grippingly personal. She could see her father, in his red tie and camel-colored coat, crouched on the sidelines like a catcher, fixed on the game in front of him, while she sat by her impeccably dressed mother, elegant in high heels and red lipstick, and two brothers, tall, sandy-haired Chris and blue-eyed Bruce. She felt invested in every down, every motion of the ball. Excitement swelled, then rushed over her like waves crashing onshore. Later, she'd describe the sport as a microcosm of life. Within its confines, you could encounter every sensation that defined the human experience: elation, joy, heartbreak, anxiety, sadness, pressure, humility, pain. As she began to meet the players and coaches, they ceased to be faceless men behind helmets. Every drop of sweat had a story behind it. The athleticism, a mixture of grit and grace, dazzled her. Her eyes began tracing the movements on the field. She felt like she belonged.

In the fading glory of the Polo Grounds, the NFL's first female scout was born.

CHAPTER 2

Not the American Bombshell

In 1950s Babylon, New York, a determined little girl lugged a briefcase of toys through her neighborhood. She had lively brown eyes and a mission as firm as her step: her parents were in trouble, and she was going to help.

Her small legs swept briskly along an unpaved path, lined with bushes, which threaded its way through a maze of yards behind her parents' house. Once a place on the Long Island shore where farmers journeyed to gather salt hay, Babylon had morphed from a glamorous resort town with the railroad's arrival to a conclave of commuters after World War II; even now, the small, friendly neighborhood was unquestionably safe to walk alone, even for a girl still in elementary school.[i]

Connie Nicholas moved fast when there was a problem to solve. Earlier that day, she'd heard her mother's soft, pleasant voice and her father's booming one mingled in a financial discussion. Pop had one of the best laughs—he'd throw back his head, and the joyous sound resonated in every corner of the room—but he hadn't been laughing then. They'd been talking about taxes. Connie had no idea what taxes were, but it sounded as if her parents didn't have enough money to pay them.

She had to do something. She grabbed an empty briefcase and began loading it with her own toys and anything else in the house that seemed sellable. Clutching her inventory, Connie let herself out the back door.

She began working her way through the neighborhood, knocking on doors, including the residence of an elderly couple one street over.

"My parents can't pay their taxes," she announced. "Would you please buy some of these toys from me to help my parents?"

From her briefcase, she drew a pair of silver toy handcuffs she used when pretending to be one of her heroes, the famous cowboy actor Roy Rogers, and offered it for sale; they politely gave her some money. Soon, the door-to-door campaign had informed more than one Babylon resident that the doctor and his wife were struggling to pay their taxes.

Back at the Nicholas home, the phone began ringing.

"You know, your daughter's going door to door selling all her toys to raise money because you can't pay your bills," a well-meaning neighbor relayed. A promising humanitarian career was quickly truncated; Connie went to bed that night reassured by her parents that they could, indeed, pay their dues to Uncle Sam. But the moment was typical of her can-do spirit and pluck, which would stay with her into adulthood and one day charm the most old-school and demanding football minds in the country. There was something mesmerizing about Connie Nicholas on a mission: you knew she wasn't going to fail.

She'd been born in nearby Levittown, Long Island, on May 31, 1951, to Dr. Calvin and Evelyn Nicholas. Two years later, the family moved to Babylon, where Dr. Cal, desiring to avoid the trap of doctors spending too much time away from their families, set up his private practice in an office in the family home—a large, welcoming two-story residence with white siding, black shutters, and a breezeway connecting the garage to the main structure. The entire purchase cost $19,000.

As a kid, Connie was cheerful and feisty, with a flair for the dramatic. When her parents squabbled, her brothers, Chris, two years older, and Bruce, four years younger, retreated to their rooms or the backyard, but Connie stood stalwart. "Pop, spank me!" she cried. "Yell at me, because you can't get divorced from *me*!" Her brothers nicknamed her "Sarah Bernhardt" (after the renowned actress) because she felt everything so passionately, except they flipped it to "Sarah Heartburn." She blazed through life with an adventuresome spirit, never sitting on her heels.

Maybe it sprang from her penchant for hero worship. *The Roy Rogers Show* was a popular children's program at the time, featuring the wholesome cowboy with the silky singing voice and powerful right hook fighting for justice in the West. Once a week, Connie and her brothers sprawled across the family room to watch a heart-pounding, 30-minute adventure in black and white flash across their TV screen. In true Connie fashion, when the Nicholas kids got a pair of plastic ponies supported on springs, Connie, bedecked in guns and holsters with a red cowboy hat perched atop her brown curls, commandeered the larger one, colored just like Rogers's famous palomino mount, Trigger, and insisted on playing the heroic cowboy—which left her younger brother in the supporting role of heroine Dale Evans, "Queen of the West," with the smaller, spotted horse. Their Uncle Jimmy—known to the rest of the world as Dr. James Nicholas, a famous orthopedist—had once operated on Rogers and promised Connie to send him over the next time he saw him. Every day, she and her friend Laurie Webster would belt out "Happy Trails," the theme song from Rogers's TV show, and run out into the Websters' front yard, anticipating that at any moment the brim of Rogers's white Stetson would appear over the horizon. Sadly, it never did, and eventually the childhood dream had to be retired. But the spirit of Rogers lingered unconsciously, fueling her earliest ideals of problem solvers, of people who could overcome anything, the ranks of the fearless. The characters that spoke to Connie were strong, adventuresome spirits who flourished in high-stakes scenarios. She never dreamed of being the lovely housewife Donna Reed, who delighted TV audiences through the '50s and '60s—that was her mother, Evelyn, whom everyone called Lynne. Connie played the cowboy, the professional baseball pitcher.

But even heroes, she proved, had vulnerabilities. All three Nicholas siblings took music lessons; Chris, who loved opera, labored through singing lessons, while Bruce and Connie went for piano. She played well—with feeling, people always said—and in private liked to tinker around, once even composing her own little moralistic tune about a "good little boy" named Chris and a "bad little boy" named Bruce in which each character received an appropriate end. But the thought of performing in a recital petrified her. She didn't want to be compared to everyone else and imagined what people would think in judgment afterwards: *Oh, she's not as good as the person who went before her.* Finally, on the day of the recital, she couldn't take it: she hid under the piano itself and stayed there, hoping to escape unnoticed. It was the only time—apart from a needle phobia—she ever hid in her life. From there on, she brokered a deal: she'd perform *only* if she could go first. When she was finally permitted to quit lessons—upon mastering "The Blue Danube" waltz—she rejoiced.

She lived a tomboy's existence. She neglected dolls, hated when her mother dressed her up, and chose to attend the rodeo over the circus every year because Roy Rogers would ride around the ring on Trigger, and fans could shake the cowboy's hand and feed treats to the famous palomino billed as "the smartest horse in the movies." One day, she answered the phone and heard a voice say, "This is Leo Durocher. Can I speak to Dr. Calvin Nicholas?" Recognizing the future Hall of Famer's name and knowing how much her father loved baseball, Connie ran screaming up to the bathroom, where Dr. Cal was taking a bath: *"Pop! Leo Durocher is on the phone!"* On discovering the caller was only a family friend having a bit of fun, her nine-year-old soul was crushed.

She even got into scrapes with her older brother. The Nicholas children were good kids, but good didn't equal *boring*. While visiting their grandmother's place in Manhattan during a bridal shower for their aunt, they felt a sudden urge to recreate a Galilean experiment: would objects of different mass fall at the same speed? Nearby—conveniently—were the coats of the guests gathered downstairs. Not long after, those same guests were treated to the fantastical sight of their coats—and whatever belongings had once populated the pockets—floating by out the window on the way to the ground. A mortified Lynne made sure her budding scientists received an appropriate punishment.

In general, however, Connie found academic topics dull; in sixth grade, she somehow landed in the advanced class and plodded through like she did every school year, wishing she were anywhere else. Her older brother, she insisted, was the brilliant one of the family, and Connie admired him for it. She preferred people to books and loved when her maternal grandfather took her and her brothers fishing in his boat, *Lola,* on the Great South Bay that stretched along the Long Island shore. "Dziadzie," as they called him[ii]—Polish for *grandfather*—had twinkling eyes, a slightly balding dome, and a rotund belly. He was always staunchly supportive of everything his granddaughter did. Sometimes she felt he was the only one who really understood her. Despite the passion with which she lived, she often felt like she was wandering through a dream, struggling to find herself or an overarching sense of purpose. And yet, Dziadzie always believed in her, as if he sensed the woman she would become, even when she had trouble believing in herself.

But the best outlet, she discovered, for her intrepid soul was sports. By the 1950s, baseball had been part of the American consciousness for decades, a morale booster during the days of World War II, and another generation of stars—their ranks swelled by those who'd put their careers on hold to serve—had succeeded the old guard of Babe Ruth and Ty Cobb in charming the sports-loving population of America, which overwhelmingly preferred it to football. The games unfolded on grainy, black-and-white TV screens that had begun populating households across the country or in the crackling sound of radio broadcasts. Wiffle ball, an offshoot of baseball that used a perforated white plastic ball, spread as the decade progressed—the ball's marketing promised curving pitches *and* safer play in confined neighborhoods.[iii] In the Nicholas backyard, Dr. Cal built a magnificent diamond to scale, using a machine that drew white lines on the dirt to construct real baselines and a batter's box. Connie, her hair often whisked back in a bun, grabbed her bat and glove and dashed out to join her brothers and their friends, playing variations of the pastime on summer evenings until darkness forced them inside. On a baseball diamond, she fit like a well-worn glove. Athletic movement, even throwing, came easily to her, and she learned quickly observing others. When it was her turn on the mound, she'd pause and look toward home plate as if reading a catcher's sign, just as she'd seen the pros do. Sometimes she tried imitating San Francisco Giants pitcher Bobby Bolin, he of the sweeping sidearm pitch, his arm gliding through the air like a hot knife through butter. At the plate, she hit better than most of the boys, with a roaring swing like big-league slugger Harmon Killebrew. The boys welcomed her talent, both in the neighborhood and later, when, during recess in sixth grade, she trooped outside with them to play baseball—the only girl in sight, yet always the first pick by one of the two captains as they selected their teams.

There, however, her athletic opportunities stopped. There were no organized girls' sports offered in her school district until high school, with the exception of a few swim teams in the area sponsored by independent organizations. Beyond that, opportunities for female athletes were scarce. During World War II, a women's baseball league had gained popularity but lost steam as the '50s progressed, collapsing in 1954. As late as 1968, the battle for women to compete as jockeys would draw a boycott and threat of a strike from men in the field. Since its inception in 1931, the Associated Press's Female Athlete of the Year had featured only golf, figure skating, tennis, water sports, and track. To be fair, there wasn't much else. Basketball had a traveling exhibition team for women, a few international competitions, and the Amateur Athletic

Union's national women's championship, yet no such title on the college circuit. Professional football was a black hole. Pro baseball had at least had two female scouts; there was no known instance of a woman ever doing such a thing in the NFL.[iv]

But it wasn't just lack of opportunity; they were also competing against an ideal. Women who participated in the Olympics were feted in issues of *Life* magazine, and yet, tucked amid the beautiful photographs touting their grace and athleticism was this quote from a fencer of 12 years, who balanced her job at a Los Angeles phone service with 12-hour-a-week practices: "Many times I think I should be in a beauty parlor getting fixed up instead." Even the women's baseball league asked their members to refrain from patronizing public bars (apparently in case they slipped through the team chaperone's fingers) and emphasized they maintain a feminine appearance. "Lipstick," the league president told a newspaper reporter, "is a must."[v] There was still a value placed on, and a strength found in, the domestic arts that overshadowed athletic accomplishments for women. "Men may do well enough in less demanding fields," one woman wrote for an opinion piece in *Life* magazine in the mid-1950s. "They can throw a ball overhand, hurl a discus about, climb an unimportant mountain. But put them down in a crowded department store at holiday time for some jolly scrimmage and they collapse at the first counter. A woman in 3-inch heels, with a tote bag weighing 10 pounds on her arms as a handicap, can outwalk a man on a shopping expedition any day— and outdance him again at night."[vi]

This status quo trickled down even to Connie, as she loitered on the Little League field with her brothers before their games, leaving the diamond only when the first pitch neared, never stopping to think if things should be otherwise. What some might view as deprivation, she took in stride. As she cheered her brothers on from the sidelines, ambitions to reshape what a girl could do in a man's world never crossed her mind. Nor did anyone tell her she couldn't; it just simply wasn't thought of.

In fact, there was only one doubter's voice she heard as she grew older: her own, which whispered critiques on the rare occasion she looked in the mirror. She was a sturdily built girl with curly hair and an oddly shaped nose. Some boys at school had nicknamed her "Captain Hook" because of it. Once, when she was much younger, she'd come home crying. Her teacher had called her ugly, she explained. Concerned, Dr. Cal and Lynne paid the teacher a visit.

"Did you tell Connie she was ugly?" they demanded.

"No, no," the teacher clarified. "I told her that *when* she sucks her thumb, she looks ugly."

But Connie's worry only grew. Struggling with poor eyesight, she began wearing glasses, which made her even more self-conscious. By the end of fifth grade, she was towering above her classmates—boys and girls—from a lofty 5'8". She felt the disparity between her own image and that of her dainty, blonde-haired mother, who glided through life with an enchanting feminine grace. Lynne Nicholas could entertain a legion of guests without a golden hair falling from its place, clean a house in high heels, bake an apple pie that made your mouth water, and was invariably feeding the neighborhood kids who trooped through her house. Her home was decorated beautifully, her taste in clothes impeccable.

And she was stunning. Crowned by her blonde hair, even her modest hemlines and necklines couldn't conceal her well-shaped legs and slender figure. Wherever she went, compliments trailed after her. "Isn't your mother beautiful," people innocently remarked to her young daughter. Connie was torn between passionate agreement and self-doubt. It seemed these people were wondering what had happened to her, why her mother was so exquisite and she was ugly. She feared, just as when she'd anticipated performing at her piano recitals, that she could never measure up. Her mother was everything a woman should be—domestic, sweet-tempered, irresistibly beautiful and devoted to her husband and children. She, meanwhile, was boisterous, ugly, and brazen—a hopeless tomboy. She felt destined to be a disappointment.

But something was stirring on the horizon. A game, fumbling through its own awkward adolescence, and an underdog team in blue and gold, were about to remake her world.

CHAPTER 3

The Football Tutor

It really began with her uncle, Dr. James Nicholas, and the strange, tragic case of Howard Glenn in the early 1960s.

The newborn decade was pulsating. A suave, impeccably coiffed John F. Kennedy was trying to convince the masses a Catholic could be president. Soviet Russia towered like a cold, calculating enemy halfway across the world. Communism had set Cuba and China ablaze and was on the cusp of building a wall in Berlin. At home, men smoked and ate dinner with the family and women smoked and dressed like Jackie Kennedy. While most heads of households had achieved only an 11th-grade education, there was still a formality of thought and appearance in the way Americans lived, a trait that would become devalued as the decade aged.[i]

Meanwhile, pro football, too old to be in its infancy, yet far from fully developed, was on the threshold of discovering its power. In 1958, a nail-biting NFL championship, later dubbed "The Greatest Game Ever

Played," had dazzled the nation. The next year, a group of men, undeterred by the 40 franchises that had crashed and burned before them, got together and decided the NFL should have some competition.[ii] One of the men was Harry Wismer, an ambitious, volatile broadcaster who received permission to establish a franchise—called the Titans—in New York for the AFL's inaugural season in 1960. But New York already had a football team, as Wismer was well aware: the long-established and well-respected Giants of the NFL.

"What is bigger than a giant?" the owner queried his new running back and punter Joe Pagliei, who'd been the last cut of the NFL Philadelphia Eagles that year and signed with Wismer's team for an annual salary of $8,500.

Pagliei answered that he didn't know.

"You sure you don't?" Wismer pressed, then continued. "A Titan is. We're gonna squash them."

His imagination, it turned out, was bigger than either. When Pagliei's wife and her friend showed up at the Polo Grounds for his first game, Pagliei was convinced they were two of only 500 people total in the stands. After the game, he turned on the shower in the locker rooms, and a hoard of "brown stuff" came pouring out. The stadium, which had been around in one form or another since 1911, was showing its age and neglect.

Nor was that the only struggle facing the Titans of New York. Handing out paychecks triggered a stampede to the bank, since no one knew how much money was actually in the account. Pagliei once had to take out a $300 loan from head coach Sammy Baugh after trying to cash his paycheck at a bank in Houston when the team was traveling, only to have the teller respond, "There are no funds in there."

But on that trip, the team experienced something far more horrific than bounced checks or meager crowds. On October 9, in a football stadium in Houston, Texas, their offensive guard, Howard Glenn, was dying. He was dying on the field, in front of 16,151 people, but nobody knew.[iii]

Maybe he didn't even know. All he said was he felt awful, like he wasn't going to make it. The heat that day was suffocating—90 degrees at the stadium. He and his New York Titans teammates had been bathed in sweat before they even stepped onto the field for warm-ups. But Glenn's condition was worse, a teammate would write later: he had foam at his mouth, and his body was exuding an odor like sewage. Finally, admitting fatigue, he left the game. In the locker room, his teammates would see a frightening sight: his 234-pound body slipped from a chair, smacking the floor underneath. Yellow-green mucus dribbled from his mouth and his pupils disappeared. His teammates tried to help, wiping the mucus off, and an ambulance came. At some point, Glenn slipped into unconsciousness—and never awoke.

The following day, a newspaper report said the cause of Glenn's death remained uncertain; doctors ruled out heat exhaustion early, and eventually, the autopsy revealed it was a broken neck, with the medical examiner claiming it had taken a while for the bone fragments to cut the spinal cord. Accounts vary as to whether the injury happened against Houston or the game prior, but later, as Glenn's teammates watched game tape, they noticed a defensive lineman had braced both hands together at the wrist and thrust upward, hitting Glenn under the chin and snapping his neck. Without a doctor to monitor the Titans on the sidelines, often the coaching staff never knew when players were really hurt in-game.[iv]

The news of Glenn's death ate at Dr. James Nicholas ("Dr. Jim" to his patients and friends), who'd earlier declined Wismer's invitation to join the organization as a team physician.[v] At the time, Dr. Jim felt he didn't have the working knowledge for the position, and financially, he couldn't afford the hours away from his private practice. But now, his conscience plagued him: Had he accepted Wismer's offer, could he have prevented the tragedy?[vi] So he reversed his decision, joined the Titans staff, and began educating himself on the sparse landscape of sports medicine, traveling to different conferences that offered courses from one of the few experts in the field, a Dr. Don O'Donoghue from the University of Oklahoma's medical school.[vii]

In September of 1962, he approached his brother, Dr. Cal, about monitoring the visitors' sidelines during a Titans home game against the Denver Broncos. The physician siblings presented a lively contrast. Trailblazing Dr. Jim, the oldest, was at home in the spotlight, with a client list that, at one point or another, featured nearly every star of his decades-long career, from Brigitte Bardot and Rudolph Nureyev to John F. Kennedy and his wife, Jackie. Dr. Cal, meanwhile, treated everyone he met like a Kennedy. He had the right kind of smile for interacting with the world: one that lit up his face and made one want to laugh along with him. His weakness, growing up, had been baseball; his brother's had been the curfew, causing their mother, Julia Nicholas, to rig a homemade alarm system of milk bottles set up just inside the door to announce when her son tried to sneak in at night. She was a single working mother whose indomitable will had pushed her children to success and yet at times felt almost suffocating (her gentle-souled ex-husband, whom she labeled "The Dreamer," had once envisioned opening a movie theater where the pictures actually talked; Julia dismissed the concept as incredibly dumb). It was she who insisted each of her three children—two boys and a girl—either marry a doctor or become one. Dr. Cal had eventually followed his brother into the medical profession, where both proved brilliant.[1]

Now, as the two men talked, Dr. Jim made working a stint on the sidelines sound easy.[viii]

"Don't worry," he assured his brother. "Just wave if you need me and I'll take care of everything for you."

And so Dr. Cal found himself sitting on a bench on the visitors' sidelines at the Polo Grounds, the same stadium where he'd once watched the boys of summer act out America's great pastime. Now a different kind of game played on the field stretched before him—a game of the future, more robust than contemplative, well matched to the briskness of autumn. It was framed this afternoon by some of the best plumage the season could offer: a brilliant sky hung overhead as the two teams battled under the September sun, the

---

[1] Dr. Cal's sister, Pat, did indeed marry a doctor.

Titans in their pale blue and gold, the visiting Denver Broncos in royal blue and blinding orange.

Suddenly, a Broncos offensive lineman, bearing down the field on a second block, took a forearm to the face. The right side of his jaw shattered, a slice of bone piercing his gum. Dr. Cal began waving his brother over.

There was no response, so he waved again.

No response.

Another wave.

No response.

Dr. Jim likely never saw the signal—he was busy enough. The Titans had been crippled since the third play from scrimmage when their starting quarterback, Lee Grosscup, hurt his left knee. The team would have eight players visit the hospital from injuries sustained during the game. Dr. Cal, meanwhile, was left to do what he could for the injured Bronco, who had a compound fracture of the jaw and underwent surgery in a New York hospital the next day. Overall, the doctor found it a rather nerve-wracking introduction to working in professional football.

But to his daughter, the development proved a boon. Dr. Cal continued monitoring the sidelines at home games, and the Nicholas family's free time soon became structured around game days at the stadium. But they didn't just go—they *embraced* it, from dainty Lynne to blue-eyed Bruce, eager to cheer on the team regardless of whatever elements or ailments (Lynne often suffered from debilitating migraines) the week threw at them. No one proved more infatuated than Connie, who, true to form, threw herself into this new environment with every tremor of her passionate soul. She yelled madly, lived and died by the final score, and gallantly defended the game's virtues to her brothers, who, despite their undeniable enthusiasm for the team, still considered baseball king. But to their sister, football had become the pinnacle. The game was faster, she argued with them; the players more athletic. Meeting the players, and watching their familiar faces storm the field on game days, thrilled her sportsman's soul. Her universe became absorbed by one thing: the game.

But as her obsession deepened, questions arose. Until now, her knowledge had been limited to whatever rules governed their neighborhood games of tackle football. There was so much she didn't know. What made a quarterback good at his craft? A defender excel at foiling a receiver?

Hungry to learn more, she turned to a family friend for help in the autumn of 1963: a local science teacher named Paul Albert, who would later scout professionally for the NFL. Connie had known Albert and his wife, Betty, for a while; they were friends of her parents, and Albert, along with coaching the varsity basketball team, taught earth science to eighth graders at Babylon Junior and Senior High, where she and Chris went to school. Only twelve, she'd yet to take a class from Albert, but she'd heard him talk with her father about football when Dr. Cal had approached him for help learning the sport. The doctor had spent most of his life as a baseball man, and now, with the Jets, found himself embroiled in a game he knew little about. To fix that, he turned to Albert, and soon invited the science teacher to camp during football's preseason when he traveled to examine the players. Sometimes, in evenings at home, Connie heard her father on the phone with Albert, talking football, as he relaxed in his recliner on the family's enclosed porch, the smoke from his cigar wafting through the air. That the daughter thought to follow in the father's footsteps ought to have been a natural progression.

But Albert better understood its rarity. He'd long been aware that, when he and the doctor talked football, the doctor's daughter was listening, too. He was a tall man, with a short haircut that meant business and clear, brown eyes that saw right through to what someone was thinking and suggested he might have a sense of humor about it. There was little Albert hadn't seen himself: he'd been a high-school dropout, a teacher, a coach, earned two master's degrees, and flown across Europe as an aerial gunner in World War II. He'd witnessed the invasion of Normandy from the skies and bombed Germany on his 21st birthday. Eventually, he settled on Long Island with his wife, Betty, and began teaching, first at a school called Westhampton Beach, then at Babylon Junior and Senior High, where Connie and Chris attended.[ix] In the classroom, he was fair, funny, but intolerant of miscreants. Once, after class, he took on a student from the wrestling team who'd given him too much lip. The fight lasted about 10 seconds—all it took for the kid to learn a lesson. His only foible appeared to be getting sidetracked from lecturing on rocks and terrains in class to discuss sports, of which his knowledge was expansive. With Connie, he was struck by what, in his experience, was an unusual interest for a young girl in athletics. But

Albert was also a fair man. This was someone, he recognized, who wanted to know more than what the score was. She wanted to know what was involved with the game.

He began answering the questions she brought most afternoons after school to his classroom. She'd settle in at one of the long, black desks in the front row, while Albert, in his suit and tie like all the faculty, perched on his desk, or sometimes headed to the blackboard, and the hand that once saved countless souls from the grip of the Nazis now scattered X's and O's across the blackboard, helping his young student visualize football concepts; later on, he continued the tutorials at football games themselves, where the two families often sat together.

Under Albert's guidance, her vision began to expand. Albert taught her to look at the different positions on the field, rather than constantly follow the ball. He knew that too many people saw only the flashy parts of the game—the run, the pass—instead of looking for what made the play happen—the block that gave the quarterback time and space to make the throw, or blazed a path for a runner. They had long conversations about personnel—what to look for when evaluating players. He dissected the skills it took to play a position like cornerback, who guarded a quarterback's targets downfield. A good cornerback couldn't stop every pass thrown in his direction, Albert explained, but he might be comfortable playing loose off a receiver because he tackled well. It was crucial for a cornerback to be a good tackler when a pass was caught two or three yards in front of him, to make the play and stop the receiver there. Otherwise, the receiver burned him twice—first by catching the ball, then by the yards he gained running with it afterward.

But their talks went deeper than just strategy. Albert knew to value the fearless defensive player, the great hitter, guys that *wanted* to be there. "That's one of the elements of football you're always looking for," he'd say later. "You're looking for the kids that are unafraid, that are real good hitters, that like to play the game."

Connie came back week after week, eager to keep learning. Albert found her an astute student and treated her as seriously as any of the football players who swung by his classroom to ask their own questions; Connie, in turn, admired Albert's quiet air of authority and vast knowledge. He never mentioned his military service to her, yet, with her penchant for hero worship, she must have sensed the heroism within. She soon idolized him along with Rogers and her favorite baseball player, San Francisco outfielder Willie Mays, one of the most electrifying athletes in the sport's history. Mays, an African American, had come of age playing baseball in the segregated South, but on reaching the majors never spent much time talking about the racial divide; he simply bridged it by playing better than everyone else.[x] He was a pioneer, not a crusader, much as Connie would one day define herself as a woman navigating the fraternity of professional scouting. Perhaps, in Mays's cheerful demeanor, the joy that exuded from him on the field, the young girl sensed a kinship of spirit, despite their disparate backgrounds.

The civil rights movement, in fact, had reached critical mass. That August, as people flooded the National Mall of Washington, D.C., Dr. Martin Luther King, Jr. had uttered the words "I have a dream" on the steps of the Lincoln Memorial. Connie and her brothers, however, had already been endowed with a powerful sense of equality, thanks to their father. Dr. Cal had a strong distaste for racial prejudice and practiced what he preached with the countless number of black and white athletes he came across, treating everyone so fairly that he earned the respect of both. Once, Chris, standing in the Jets locker room, saw a player whom he considered a leader of the African Americans on the team—a defensive back not necessarily given to flattery—look at his father and say approvingly, "Doc, you're OK."

In fact, their father's intolerance of any discrimination, whether ethnic or religious, affected Connie and her siblings down to where they swam during the summer. It wasn't uncommon in the area for Jews to be excluded from yacht club memberships, and though Dr. Cal was Greek Orthodox, several of his medical colleagues were Jewish. At some point, he refused to keep patronizing a club with such a policy, and so in 1962, he enrolled his family at the newer Long Island Yacht Club up the street. It was an inclusive but extremely unglamorous affair, with an oddly shaped pool that looked like a kidney.

But its existence opened a new world for Connie: actual athletic competition, since yacht club swim teams were open to boys and girls. Though she'd never taken a formal swim lesson, she'd learned the basics somewhere—so casually that she didn't even remember from whom—and decided to join the team anyway. Her plan carried a noticeable handicap: on reaching the pool wall, she had no idea how to execute a flip turn, unlike her competition, and instead had to grab the wall with her hand. A good stroke and overall speed saved her, and she frequently won. Mr. Duart, the coach, made her believe in herself and, under his guidance, Connie felt herself develop as an athlete. She also developed a crush; Mr. Duart was tall, irresistibly good-looking, and—the clincher—had played football at Auburn.

Joining the club, she found, had been good for her socially: the other kids were welcoming, and she started attending multiplication dances that were held there. One boy and one girl would start on the dance floor, then they'd go and grab two more people, who'd go and grab two more, till eventually, everyone was out on the floor and no one had to fear being without a partner.

Swept up in a myriad of new pursuits, Connie felt she'd come alive at last. As she sat in her bedroom one day, with its blue flowered wallpaper, strumming her guitar, she had the sensation of waking, of life taking on a new vibrancy. Football, the yacht club—everything was falling into place. No longer did life hold the drowsiness of adolescence adrift. She'd found her niche, something she could pour her heart into.

My life is beginning now, she thought.

CHAPTER 4

A Guy Named Joe

Meanwhile, she watched her football team struggle to find itself. The club had yet to turn a winning season and, dogged by tumultuous finances, had filed for bankruptcy before Sonny Werblin and a purchasing group rescued it for $1 million in 1963. Under the new ownership, the team was rechristened the New York Jets and given the colors green and white to replace the old blue and gold. That summer at training camp, to emphasize structure and prepare for an afternoon photo session with the media, new head coach Weeb Ewbank began the first morning of on-field work with his players going over the most basic of football concepts: how to huddle properly at the pro level. Formerly NFL coach of the year, the short, spherical Ewbank had conveyed optimism when he took the job: "I've seen sicker cows than this get well," he'd declared.[i] But building a football team, like Rome, was not the work of a day; the Jets finished Ewbank's first season with five wins, eight losses, and a tie—the exact record they'd had the previous year.

But it wasn't just their losing that irked new owner Sonny Werblin. They were boring when they did it. Werblin came from Hollywood and had his own ideas about building a sustainable football team. "I always believed in the star system," he once declared, proving his thinking at the time was arguably bigger than the sport he was in. "I wanted a star."[ii] At training camp in 1964, he perused the assembled players, trying to find one who might do.[iii]

That season, his team was also finally able to move into its new home at Shea Stadium, feted by the press as one of the top stadiums in the country and almost unprecedented in its binary construction for baseball and football.[iv] Shifting the venue to its football layout required rearranging chunks of seats along the sidelines via two huge underground tracks. The grandeur of its architecture, however, couldn't mask a few flaws. Some creative adolescents discovered a way past the ticket office: they'd hop a stadium fence, duck under a set of bleachers, and wait for the crowds to come, then slip from their hiding place and mingle with the suckers who actually paid for admittance. Football fans were also subject to the frigid wind that sometimes rushed uninvited off nearby Flushing Bay and transported the crowd to a biting tundra. In the stands, even diehard Connie noticed the chill from the stadium's cold concrete surface creep through her boots, penetrating her skin until it mingled with the nerves that clutched her muscles, making them tense and primed like a band waiting to snap. Chris sometimes wrapped plastic bags around his feet to keep them warm. But the team's losses hurt more than the elements—they cut at places the wind couldn't reach and made Connie's Mondays at school even more unbearable.

Feeling the pallor of his team's brand, Sonny Werblin decided to raise the stakes.

On a night in late January, 1965, a young man waited in a New York hospital. He had a strong arm, broad features, Hollywood charisma, and a new boss who knew how to market it. Swap new cinema icon James Bond's Walther PPK for a football, and you got a vision of what this young man could become: an idol of the gridiron *and* the glamorous.

Just a few weeks earlier, he'd been sitting at a desk, posing with a groundbreaking contract to play quarterback for the Jets. Papers swirled with rumors of the reported salary—numbers ranged from $389,000 to $427,000, over 17 times greater than the average player salary even four years later—but what everyone generally agreed on was this: it was likely the biggest rookie contract ever seen in professional football. Ironically, the young man had entered the room for a press conference to acknowledge the signing in a new jacket and tie, but with a hole in the sole of his right shoe.[v] The misstep would soon be forgotten—he had too much star quality for the detail to stick.

And star quality, Werblin knew, was exactly what his team needed.

What the owner likely *didn't* know was that the star he'd chosen, the young buck now sitting in the hospital room, had spent part of his childhood playing it low-key—at least, that's how he saw it—as the youngest of several siblings. "I wasn't out in front," he'd say later. "I was a quiet guy."

Despite that, the boy, named Joe Namath, was thrilled the first time he saw his name in the paper as part of a Little League box score. Before he was done playing football at the University of Alabama, he'd appeared to master a comfort with the spotlight that his athleticism deserved and his charisma demanded. Namath practically majored in swagger. In the bathroom one morning, his teammates brushing their teeth, Namath recycled a line he'd once heard a Navy veteran use back in Beaver Falls, PA. "I can't wait for tomorrow, 'cause I get better looking every day," Namath declared, looking in the mirror. It was the first time he'd used the line publicly, and it had great effect.

It was, in fact, a stroke of genius that the second-class Jets had managed to land Namath in the 1965 draft. At the time, top college players were often wooed by the AFL and the NFL, and competition between the leagues proved fierce. By the following draft, the NFL would have a legion of volunteer "babysitters" across the country who served as league ambassadors and kept an eye on top talent to prevent their being dazzled into signing with the AFL.[vi] In one case, a sitter jetted off on the honeymoon with a newlywed player and his wife, guarding their marriage certificate in his pocket; this was after he'd been to their rehearsal and wedding and aided in organizing the honeymoon. In New York, the NFL set up a top-secret control room, secured by detectives, where sitters could call and spill information to men known as "supervisors." The supervisors wrote up players' demands and quirks on blackboards, or competing offers from the AFL (the Broncos, for example, threw in a deal sweetener for one player to get his girlfriend a job at a beauty shop). The room also had ambassadors from the 15 NFL teams, who digested the information for their respective clubs' needs. One sitter lost out big-time—his player went missing. He'd been "kidnapped," so to speak, by the AFL, though the incident was so casual that a *Life* reporter and a photographer were invited along to chronicle the player and AFL tycoon Lamar Hunt driving to an airport and boarding a plane. Still, the disappearance was unexpected enough that the player's mother frantically called the NFL control room to find out what happened to her son, only presumably to discover, along with the league when the plane landed, that he'd signed with the AFL en route. At the Nicholas house, for fun, Dr. Cal kept score by writing down each draft pick and the league he chose on a series of file cards, with Connie and her brothers rooting madly for the AFL to triumph. Since the drafts weren't televised, Dr. Cal searched for player updates in *The Sporting News*, published weekly.

Namath's signing, however, made headlines. The heralded collegiate quarterback had also been drafted by the NFL St. Louis Cardinals that winter, yet chose the parvenu AFL for his playing career. "A tremendous prestige factor," one newspaper claimed for the league.[vii]

But there was a catch on which all his—and the team's—potential glory hinged: an operation to repair the young man's knee, which he'd damaged in college and was bad enough to keep him from being drafted into the Vietnam War.[viii] Werblin hoped at least to salvage it for a football career. That task now fell directly into the hands of Connie's uncle, Dr. Jim. The future of the Jets franchise was suddenly resting on her family—an unforeseen effect of the profession her grandmother had imposed on her sons so many years before.

In fact, the night before his surgery, Namath received a visit from the formidable, dark-haired matriarch herself, who was visiting a sick grandchild in the same hospital. She even gave the quarterback a gift: a medal of St. Jude, traditionally patron of impossible tasks, and a more interesting choice than Julia Nicholas herself might have known. When Namath was playing basketball in sixth grade, he and a seventh grader named Richie found themselves the two smallest kids on the team. The boys, who attended Catholic school, had been studying various saints and identified a perfect opportunity to apply their newfound knowledge. Two pleas for growth spurts were sent up to St. Jude, who put Namath on a delayed gratification plan, indulging his request between sophomore and junior year of high school. (Richie, unfortunately, wasn't quite as successful.) But by the time Namath reached the Jets, St. Jude had amply repaid his trust: the quarterback stood at a lofty 6'2".

Now, right before the biggest surgery of his life, the saint had surfaced again.

The quarterback thanked Connie's grandmother, while privately—and half-jokingly—wondering if she knew something about her son's medical aptitude that he didn't. Had the doubt ever existed in earnest, it would have evaporated over the next 11 years, as Dr. Jim coaxed wins, records, and shocking longevity out of the dilapidated knee. Running the day of the surgery was a print cartoon that imagined head coach Ewbank and owner Werblin pacing the hospital hall. "Any word from Dr. Nicholas?" Werblin is saying. Later, Connie got the owner to sign a copy of the cartoon. "To Connie," he wrote, "with great appreciation for all that your father and uncle are doing for us." Meanwhile, during Namath's visit back to Alabama in February, over a hundred people defied a downpour to welcome him at the airport, where he good-naturedly smooched a stewardess three times for photographers.[ix]

"FOOTBALL GOES SHOW BIZ" blazed the *Sports Illustrated* headline on the team that summer of 1965, as Namath and his teammates practiced up at Peekskill Military Academy. The food was terrible and the beds the players slept in were so small they had to stick their feet through the bars on the endboard just to lie full-length. But it was the only prep school that accepted one of the Jets owners' sons, so the team held training camp there every summer. Connie, visiting with her family over the years, easily rattled off players' names and their alma maters as she stood on the sidelines. One trip, decked out in her green and white sundress, with a pink headband holding back her brown curls, she got her picture taken with Namath. As he rested one forearm on her shoulder, his other hand tucked casually in his pocket, he exuded effortless cool; Connie, behind her cat-eye sunglasses, hung right with him, though a big smile revealed her elation. Her guileless enthusiasm for football won him over quickly, a remarkable feat, considering how often he encountered enthused fans. By the end of the decade, to know Namath was like knowing the Beatles, who swept across America on tour in the summer of 1965 and filled the air with their innovative harmonies and universal lyrics. "You really know Joe Namath?" people began asking Connie that year.

Werblin had found his superstar.

CHAPTER 5

The Girl Without a Date

That fall, Connie was finally eligible to try out for girls' sports at school, though technically, ninth graders were still considered part of the junior high. In general, Babylon Junior and Senior High treated female athletics as an afterthought. It fell to the girls' head basketball coach, Charlotte Sohl, to figure out her team's playing schedule, find referees to officiate games, arrange buses for transportation, and make sure the school gym was available—or at least half of it, since that's all the girls were allotted for both games and practices (the boys were awarded the whole space). The girls' team even scrounged for basketballs, since they received only two new ones a year. The boys, meanwhile, had baskets full of them, so any time they negligently allowed one to slip, forgotten, behind the bleachers, Sohl snatched it and wrote "girls" in magic marker over the surface. The boys never missed them.

Sohl's teams, in fact, were often quite good. An attractive brunette, she knew sports forwards, backwards, and inside out; she coached basketball and softball, officiated, and helped judge aspiring referees as part of their certification process. She also taught physical education classes at the school, which at that time were segregated by gender. Connie joined the row of girls in their one-piece, button-down white gym suits, with their last name on the pocket, as Sohl blew a whistle. “Attention!” Sohl announced, and their hands dropped to their sides. “Dress, right, dress,” she commanded.

Connie slid her left hand up to her waist so that her elbow stuck out, like the other girls—the idea was to form a line with equal spaces between each person. When this had been accomplished, Sohl cried, “At ease,” and the girls put their hands behind their backs and stood with their feet apart while she took attendance. Girls on the basketball team wore those gym suits for games, underneath an odd-looking, sleeveless, short tunic called a pinny, which tied at the waist and sported a playing number.

Her first year, Connie made varsity in the four main sports available to female students—basketball, field hockey, volleyball, and softball. She dropped field hockey after two years because she found the pressure of goaltending ridiculous. In basketball, her height was finally an asset; she had the advantage on layups and was also a terrific foul and outside shooter. Sohl worked with her to get the ball down low to the other stationary forward, Ethel Wickham, for an easy layup. “He who hesitates is guarded,” she’d tell Connie and the other forwards, emphasizing the need to anticipate their next move with the ball. The girls weren’t thought to have the stamina for 5-on-5-play, or "boys' rules," as it was called, so they played six-player basketball: two forwards, anchored in the opponent's end and forbidden by rules to move past half-court; two guards, restricted to the defensive zone; and two rovers, able to traverse the whole playing area. Their games were relegated to the afternoon, often poorly attended, and viewed by the school more as social events than serious competition. After they finished playing, both teams gathered on the field or in the school cafeteria to introduce themselves over milk and cookies—or donuts and cider during field hockey season—before heading home.

There was one fan, however, who never missed a game: Lynne Nicholas, who staunchly supported her daughter's athletic endeavors. She even helped the mother of another swimmer, Robert Russell, with meets down at the yacht club—accessorized in red, white, and blue to match the swim team's colors, and crowned by their golden hair, they were the prettiest mothers there. During high-school games, Lynne was a fixture in the stands or on the sidelines, cheering the athletes on, while Dr. Cal made sure he filmed every event; the film was silent but the gesture endearing. Their presence demonstrated rare support at the time for Babylon's female athletes.

But even immersed—at last—in sports at school, Connie made time for football. From the sofa in her family's enclosed porch, she studied the limited number of games televised on weekends in the New York market: Jets' and Giants' away games and the one college contest broadcast by ABC on Saturday afternoons during the regular season. If Jets defensive coach Walt Michaels stopped by the Nicholas house when a college game happened to be on, he'd watch with her—she was always ready to learn, the tough-as-nails coach observed. Other times, Connie watched with Paul Albert, if he and Betty were visiting. Beginning in 1965, Dr. Cal had bought over a dozen tickets in Shea Stadium's Section 17, which meant Connie often sat next to the Alberts when the Jets played at home, dissecting the games with Paul during timeouts. On days she wasn't playing sports, she kept up her visits to his classroom, eager to talk football.

Around her, the world was changing. The country seemed caught up in a sort of teenage angst—as if it didn't know its identity, or where it was going.[i] It wasn't just the Beatles; there was the swing of Motown and the crooning of an aging Sinatra, mingled with the edginess of his daughter's smash single, "These Boots Are Made for Walking." Andy Warhol's art depicted celebrities and the commonplace in hues so vivid they could have roused the devotees of the burgeoning drug culture. There was a war on everything: a war on poverty, a war in Vietnam, a Cold War. What was once informal was becoming regimented—in 1966, Congress permanently codified Daylight Saving Time—and what was once formal soon became lax: love, fashion. Spreads in *Life* magazine featured pantsuits and their cousin, the "shortsuit"; more than one restaurant debated if they should accept trouser-clad female patrons at all.[ii] In the halls of Babylon High, it didn't matter, as girls were already forbidden from wearing pants to school; the boys, meanwhile, inspired by the Beatles and subsequent "British Invasion," grew their hair into long, shaggy mops. Connie preferred a more traditional vibe—she liked the wholesome serenader Andy Williams, who charmed the country with his dulcet rendition of "Moon River."

Privately, she'd yet to solve her old, nagging qualms about her appearance. The silky, straight locks of the latest "it" girl, a youthful Cher, had Connie chafing at her natural curls, which she chopped into a short '60s 'do. She would have loved to go on a date, but nobody asked. She went to one dance, and that was only because it was a Sadie Hawkins dance, where the girl invites the guy. Connie, in a gesture of friendship, had asked dark-haired Vinnie O'Shea from the school's football team. He was so tall that, even with her bouffant, the tip of her brunette hair barely grazed his eye level. They stood awkwardly shoulder-to-shoulder in her parents' living room, facing the camera. He'd pinned a white corsage to her shoulder, but the arms hanging at his sides as they posed betrayed a lack of tender interest.

In general, her lack of a boyfriend proved a problem she was at a loss to solve. Her personality wasn't naturally flirtatious, or alluring, and no matter what, her nose wasn't going to get better. She was generally oblivious to things like fashion; her maternal grandmother, Mimi, sewed some of her clothes, and, while people at Babylon High thought her wardrobe beautiful, Connie herself was the least likely to remember what someone had been wearing—she was far more interested in the fit of major league pitcher Al Jackson's baseball glove. So far, that trait had failed to captivate her male peers at school.

But she was good at connecting with people. When Clyde Davis moved with his family in 1967 to an all-white Babylon neighborhood, he found himself one of the only black students at the high school—a shock after coming from an African American neighborhood in Queens. Cautious and slightly apprehensive as he processed his new surroundings, he was befriended by the entire Nicholas family, including this football-crazed girl who always seemed to be wearing green and white. They were the only colors that mattered, as the teenagers talked about their weekends and discussed the Jets. Kids at school knew Connie was the daughter of a Jets doctor, but she was also outgoing in her own right—a bubbly, brown-eyed girl with a nice smile. Even Joe Namath, the first time they met, felt comfortable around her. By that time, he'd gotten to know Dr. Cal and inferred a similar vibe with his daughter, as if he could divine the warmth and sincerity within.

But at home, it was a different story. Connie and her father had similar temperaments, and when they clashed—which they did frequently—it was a full-fledged tempest; once, as a little girl, she'd led him in a chase around the dining room table, taunting, "I'm not gonna cry!" in anticipation of an imminent spanking. They'd bellow and rage; Dr. Cal had a unique way of arguing wherein he never held grudges, so he refused to dredge up past grievances and stuck to the topic at hand, throwing the full force of his Greek passion behind it. But Connie, equally strong-willed, would rather be spanked than be silent; she rolled her eyes, talked back, or challenged his opinions even if she agreed with them, impishly unable to let Pop have his lecture. The doctor's most effective weapon dealing with her was often a simple question: "Do you want to be like every other woman, or do you want to be like your mother?" he'd demand. That usually slowed her down—Connie wanted desperately to be like her mother and already feared she never would.

One morning, not long before starting high school, she traipsed downstairs in a sour mood and turned into the kitchen. Dr. Cal, who always sat in a corner chair, reading the newspaper over scrambled eggs and toast, noticed her attitude and launched into a lecture.

"There is no reason why, when you get up in the morning, you come down the stairs, and you come to breakfast, you can't have a smile on your face and say 'Good morning' and be happy," he observed. "All you have to do is go to school. All we ask is that you get good grades, and enjoy something, whether it's sports or arts or whatever you're going to enjoy. We don't ask you to do errands. We don't ask you to do chores." (This was true—Lynne handled most of the day-to-day housework, arguing that the kids had the rest of their lives to work and that she'd rather they have the time growing up to pursue hobbies they loved, like music or sports.)[iii]

"I want you to go back upstairs," Dr. Cal continued. "And until you're going to do that every morning, I don't want you coming down."

On a normal morning, Connie would have just scowled harder. But this time, something in her father's tone made her realize he meant business. Stunning Chris, who witnessed the incident, she climbed back up the steps.

At the top, she paused for as long as she could. To go back down and admit defeat—oh, that would be a bitter pill to swallow. On the other hand, if she held out too long, she'd be late for school.

One step after another, wisdom and her feet carried her back downstairs. When she reached the kitchen, her surrender became complete: she sprung a greeting that would have cheered a graveyard on Halloween.

From that day on, Connie began to look at life differently: though the fiery blowups continued, she began to focus on her blessings, not her disappointments. Her sunny outlook graduated to a conscious decision, rather than just a natural inclination. As an adult, the lilt in her voice, and her upbeat demeanor, would prove her most memorable features.

CHAPTER 6

The Men Behind the Helmets

To Connie, the best part about high school was her family's growing camaraderie with the Jets. As early as her eighth-grade year, players had begun swinging by her father's home office when they needed medical attention, apart from Sundays and eventually Tuesdays, the two days Dr. Cal had off from his private practice to work with the team. The players sometimes stayed for the coffee and cake Lynne kept on hand for such occasions, and soon the Nicholas social circle expanded to several Jets and their families. Connie and her brothers threw the whole neighborhood into the bargain—they brought players to the yacht club or engaged them in Wiffle ball contests in the backyard. The Jets players and personnel returned the hospitality: when wide receiver George Sauer, inspired by the Nicholas backyard, built his own Wiffle ball field and brought his teammates over for a game, Connie and her brothers were included, too. She discovered that, while people can root for a team without a personal connection, having a positive encounter with a player, or a coach, made it almost impossible *not* to. It was one thing to know a sport, but another to know the men who played it—to realize the humanity behind the helmets.

In a way, they became like family, their influence stretching far beyond Sunday and into the daily minutiae of her life. Sometimes, when Sauer played the guitar during visits, she accompanied him on the dark-wooded piano that sat in a corner of her parents' living room. Once, knowing how much she liked country artist Glen Campbell, he got her concert tickets for her birthday and took her backstage to meet the singer. Sauer's tall, athletic body balanced a mind that never seemed to rest; he enjoyed intellectual pursuits and, though he never spoke of it to Connie, felt playing pro football could trivialize or degrade a man. But football had been a family business; his father was a front office man, and Sauer grew up yoked under the burden of bloodline, his academic mind betrayed by his athletic limbs.[i] He seemed to find peace, however, in the fun-filled, innocent Nicholas home and was a frequent guest with his wife, the more effervescent Janet. The Nicholas kids figured out one way to entertain Sauer and other professional athletes during visits was to bring out board games; the players usually couldn't turn down a chance to compete at something. Sauer, however, would play anything: basketball on the blacktop just outside the Nicholas kitchen window, hockey in the Nicholas basement, doubles in tennis with Connie at the yacht club—she even devised hand signals so they could tip each other off when one planned to rush the net or hang back—along with Wiffle ball in the backyard. Chris and Bruce—who, like their sister, knew how to include everyone—permitted a young neighbor named Jack Catalano to stand in as official catcher while the older boys played. During one game, with Sauer at the plate, Jack—in awe of the famed visitor—tried to throw the ball back to the mound and instead plunked the wide receiver in the back.

But Sauer merely laughed.

"You know," he observed, "I have been hit by pitchers a few times, but never a catcher ... you're the first."

Dark-haired Gerry Philbin, Connie's favorite player to watch on defense, was another frequent guest. She liked watching him on Sundays because, though technically undersized for a defensive end, he played tough. She didn't know he'd been even smaller in college, weighing only 205 pounds at the end of his junior year. At the time, weight workouts were viewed suspiciously for professional athletes; the thought was that it would bind their muscles, decreasing their speed and hurting their mobility. The University of Buffalo, where Philbin attended, had, at best, a weight room as "big as your closet," he described. But Philbin, desperate for an edge that would allow him to play pro football, let a guy he knew put him in touch with a local gym owner. Three days a week, Philbin took two busses to get to his gym and lift. He also began drinking protein shakes—made of raw egg, ice cream, protein powder, and Energol (a linseed oil)—whenever he lifted. Within five months, he'd added 30 muscular pounds.

An assistant coach at the University of Buffalo named Buddy Ryan wasn't pleased.

"If you've lost any speed, you've got to lose that weight," he warned Philbin.

But Philbin not only gained strength from his new regimen, he returned to football faster than before. His senior year, all the players at the University of Buffalo began lifting weights in the big weight room the school now provided. Even the basketball coach sent his players down to lift, an act little short of a miracle, since the basketball world viewed weight training with even more skepticism than the football community. Philbin, meanwhile, was drafted by three professional football teams—the NFL Detroit Lions, the Toronto Argonauts, and the AFL New York Jets—and, liking New York City and the team ownership, he joined the Jets in 1964. In the off-season, he worked as a printing salesman to supplement his football salary and stayed in shape by a diet of sit-ups and pushups, lifting weights, or running a mile or two at the local track. Even that was beyond any off-season training the Jets required at the time, since they actually required nothing. The fact the team had training camp at all was to get players back in shape from an off-season of beer drinking. That, however, didn't seem to be Philbin's problem. The first time he and his wife, Trudy, came to the Nicholas house for dinner—it was also the first time a player had come to the house for a meal—the legacy the broad-shouldered, well-spoken defensive end left behind had nothing to do with football: it was, instead, the copious amount of milk he consumed that evening. Connie was stunned. It was all she could recall later of the event, that she'd never seen a person drink so much milk in her life. It was superhuman—and humanizing.

None of the players, however, made her teenage heart pound like wide receiver Bake Turner. There was something about the tall Texan with a charming drawl, known for holding a guitar when he wasn't cradling a football. Chris respected him, too, because he was always kind to the ball boys (as a ball boy himself for three summers with the team, Chris judged players not only by their on-field abilities, but by how they treated his brotherhood). Bake, for his part, was a real gentleman. Born in 1940, he'd note later that movies had been integral to his athletic career. Growing up, he'd watched the black-and-white *Jim Thorpe—All-American* and been inspired; though Thorpe played several sports and eventually helped establish the NFL, he'd also been an Olympic track man and had run across the countryside as a boy. So Bake started running across pastures and jumping fences. When he was older, some colleges came down to Alpine, Texas, to recruit him for their football programs. Bake found himself leaning toward Texas A&M over Texas Tech, believing A&M would give him a better shot at making the pros.

Bake's father pulled him aside.

"You know, A&M is not co-educational," he cautioned, as Bake told the story years later, slightly embellished.

"Well, I only need one education, don't I?" Bake replied.

"No, that's not what I mean," his dad answered. "They don't have any ladies at Texas A&M."

Bake signed with Texas Tech.

His foray into pro football began as uncertainly as some of its early franchises. At the Blue-Grey college all-star game in Montgomery, Alabama, pro scouts watched him catch, kick, and play defense, and even though the Baltimore Colts drafted him into the NFL, Bake instead signed with the Calgary Stampedes of the Canadian League, which almost a decade earlier had siphoned off several NFL players.[ii] But Bake's Canadian League career was brief: he was cut by Calgary early enough to make it to Colts camp that summer and scored a touchdown the first time he touched the ball during a Baltimore game. Baltimore's head coach soon received a telegraph from Calgary's general manager: "Keep him out when you're on national television, for gosh sake, or I'll get fired."[iii] The next year, the Colts cut Bake anyway, so he signed with the AFL New York Titans and led the team in receiving yards that season.

When he came to New York, the guitar came with him, even to the team's annual Thanksgiving dinner celebration at Shea Stadium's Diamond Club, which often featured live music. The event was a favorite on the Jets' calendar. Players' kids ran around, families were introduced, and everyone ate of the feast, which during the 1966 season boasted cranberry sauce, turkey, pumpkin pie, sweet potatoes, and stuffing, with shrimp cocktail, heart of lettuce, cauliflower polonaise, creamed white onions, and French-cut beans. Connie, in her element, would snap pictures with Joe, listen to Bake play and sing, and soak in the camaraderie of what, to her, had become family. At some point, she unconsciously began introducing herself to people with the phrase, "Hi, I'm Connie Nicholas. My father is the doctor for the Jets"—as if the association had become an extension of her last name.

Here, too, she got positive reinforcement. In an era when women journalists were banned from locker rooms, it was incredible access for a girl who loved sports to the kind of insight and reflections these men could offer. Namath considered her one of the first—if not the first—girl he'd met that seemed sincerely interested in football. She was always querying Philbin about different teammates or the Jets' opponents; she hung around whenever players visited the house, chatting, mostly about football. They, in turn, were surprised by her knowledge—Bake found it novel and refreshing talking with a girl who knew the rules, plays, referee hand signals, even what to expect from different teams. He felt what Albert had experienced—she didn't just want to giggle about superficial football concepts. She wanted to know the sport from the inside out.

In fact, she tried an avant-garde experiment before the '68 football draft, which at the time typically failed to generate significant media predictions, or even analysis, in the run-up to the event. For fans trying to figure out which college players might succeed as pros, information was scarce. *Street & Smith's* magazine was arguably the premiere publication and supplied football savants—from a teenage Connie, scouring its pages at home, all the way up to a team owner—with relevant information about the collegiate talent pool. "Broncos owner Bob Howsam," the *Denver Post* once wrote, "showed up at the first-ever AFL draft armed not with an army of scouts, but a copy of *Street & Smith's* magazine."

This time, on one of its pages, Connie made a mark next to a player's name: Ron Yary, an offensive tackle from the University of Southern California, who'd won the Knute Rockne Award for being the best lineman in the nation. By a second name, she made another mark: Garrett Ford, a running back from West Virginia. These, she'd decided, were her top draft picks for 1968.

She proved only partially successful. The Minnesota Vikings chose Yary first overall that year; he played in seven Pro Bowls and eventually made the Hall of Fame. Ford went in the third round and was a bust. It was, however, her first mock draft—in an era where almost no one did them.

But when it came to scouts themselves, she knew virtually nothing. It was a shadow profession, filled by people comfortable away from the spotlight. Though Connie lived and breathed a Jets life, she never recollected coming across scouts, or interacting with them, before graduating high school. It was doubtful she even knew of their existence.

CHAPTER 7

A Year to Remember

The ideal of female beauty at that time in Babylon was the blonde, frail heroine, which, by her senior year in 1968, Connie had established herself as anything but. Generally so positive, she struggled to find anything redeeming about her body, unhappy with her athletic build. At some point, Lynne, trying to be helpful, suggested a simple beauty trick like wearing lipstick. Feeling rebellious, Connie refused. Privately, she despaired. She never completely revealed her insecurity to her friends but worried she'd never find a boy who could love her.

Not that it slowed her down. She'd joined the student newspaper as girls' sports editor, played varsity volleyball, basketball, and softball her junior and senior years, and even found time to support the school gymnastics and football teams. She described herself as "happy with life" for a personality profile published in the school newspaper (her nose made the profile as one of her dislikes, along with things like Orphan Annie, the New York Giants, and getting nervous). And, of course, it was Jets all the time. "The Jets," Sohl said, "were the highlight of her life."

In fact, something strange happened to the team that fall of her senior year. They started winning—a lot.

It had taken till the previous season for the franchise to secure its first winning record, even with—or sometimes, in spite of—Namath's arm, which showcased a propensity for interceptions along with sensational strength. He was also prone to off-the-field distractions, so in 1968, the players elected him offensive captain, thereby forcing him to be more accountable.[i] Once Namath got on the field, however, the concern shifted. Defensive coordinator Walt Michaels thought the quarterback tried to do *too* much, passing when he didn't need to, throwing as if the Jets' entire game plan relied on it. It didn't. The Jets had the top defense in the league. If the team wanted to win, Michaels felt, Namath had to share that responsibility, not shoulder it alone.

It was easier said than done. Not that Namath disagreed with the analysis. In fact, when a fuming Michaels chewed him out on the topic during a team plane ride after a loss to the Buffalo Bills, Namath was man enough to admit, during an interview several years later, "I agreed with him."[ii] Yet patterns established over three seasons weren't going to vaporize instantly. He had already proven his physical talent—an AFL Rookie of the Year award in 1965 and the record he set two years later of hitting 4,000 passing yards during a single season. But it was a testament to his desire to win—that at heart, when one peeled back the celebrity, he was as much a gosh-darn competitor as the next guy—that Namath began adjusting his play. The game, after all, has never defined greatness as an absence of failure, but the power to overcome it.

And that 1968 season, the Jets defined resiliency. A bounce-back win after losing to Denver in Week 5 put them on a four-game roll; they also closed out the season with a four-game winning streak, finishing 11–3. It brought them, for the first time, to the doorstep of the 1968 AFL championship game, held on December 29 against the Oakland Raiders in the curving embrace of Shea Stadium.

The crowd that day was electric—they roared so loudly during player introductions that the PA announcer's voice was inaudible.[iii] The weather, meanwhile, had done its best to make the day inhospitable. The wind whipped off nearby Flushing Bay and patrolled the grounds like an invisible menace, toying with the football and tormenting the players. Below Connie, the field was lumpy and looked frozen.[iv] In the early years, the Nicholas family arrived outside the stadium by 9:30 a.m. for a 1 p.m. kickoff, and while Dr. Cal went in to examine the players, the rest of the family waited in the chill, bundled in their Sunday best. They'd rather stay out there till the gates opened than presume to ask for preferential treatment merely because they had a family member on staff. Now, even though their arrival time hadn't changed, the head coach's wife, Lucy Ewbank, always made sure Mrs. Nicholas and her children were invited with other spouses into the waiting room just inside the stadium.

Connie had spent the buildup to this game hijacked by nerves. The prior week, the Raiders had pummeled the Kansas City Chiefs 41–6. Pitted against them now were names as familiar as her own: Sauer, Philbin, running back Emerson Boozer, linebacker Ralph Baker, and so many more, including the dashing quarterback, still with unmistakable swagger despite his mud-spattered uniform.

The wind that day had made him a man in need of redemption. He and his team were driving in the fourth quarter when it merrily intercepted the ball, dangling it in front of an Oakland defender, who pulled it in. Namath chased him down, lowered his right shoulder, caked in mud, and lunged at him. The tackle only postponed the bleeding. The Raiders scored on their next drive and snatched the lead.

But Namath and his best receiver, Don Maynard, had conferred earlier that game.

"Joe, I got a long one when you need it," Maynard had promised.[v]

And so, on the next drive, with the defense in perfect coverage for the call, Namath, in a feat of stunning athleticism, sent the ball arcing through the air downfield and into Maynard's outstretched arms.

The Jets lined up, the goal line now just six yards away. The ball snapped. Namath saw his first receiver was covered. His second option, Sauer, had excellent receiving hands—but they might as well have been tied behind his back, so close were Oakland defenders. Oakland had negated his third receiver, too. But there was Maynard again—he'd found a peephole of hope in the back of the end zone. Namath fired, and the ball reached Maynard's hands just before he tumbled to the ground. The Jets regained the lead, 27-23. "Not many quarterbacks," Sauer observed after the game, "can hit their fourth receiver."[vi]

But now the invaders were driving. They drove all the way down field, stopped only 26 yards away from the end zone. On their next possession, they drove again, drove as if nothing could stop them—not the Jets defense, their green-and-white uniforms spattered with mud, nor the elements themselves. Completion. Gain. Completion. Gain. The Jets' goal line came into focus. The defense, so good throughout the year, now seemed hapless to protect their lead.

Fear welled up in Connie—that feeling of dread that comes when defeat is no longer a vague, distant concept, but feels chillingly imminent.

The game clock had drained to 2:20 as the ball snapped. Oakland's quarterback looked to his right, flipping it back to an intended receiver.

Then came the mistake.

Connie could see it from where she sat. The ball was thrown backwards—it was a lateral pass, not a forward pass, which meant the uncaught ball, now skipping merrily over the ground, was fair game to be scooped up by the Jets players who rushed toward it. The green-and-white-clad Ralph Baker swept it up and began running the opposite way, back toward Oakland's end zone. Back then, however, a player was not allowed to advance a ball overturned on a lateral pass, so while Baker ultimately didn't score, he also didn't need to. The defense held once more on the Raiders' final possession and, moments later, the Jets were AFL champions.

It was the biggest football game Connie had ever witnessed, a moment cemented as one of the franchise's greatest victories on home soil. The Jets and their fans would forever be trying to get back here, to the success they achieved on December 29, 1968. Yet their triumph, even in that moment, was incomplete. The team had one game left to play as the calendar turned to January—a showdown against the NFL in Miami. The game offered both a challenge and a chance: to erase the second-class label that had dogged the AFL for so long, and to even the balance of power in professional football between the two leagues. As Connie packed her bags for the trip to Miami, she had no assurance which one awaited her: historic victory or heartbreaking defeat.

On the afternoon of January 12, 1969, overcast skies hung over Miami's Orange Bowl Stadium. Palm trees framed the view behind the giant scoreboard. Tucked among the mass of 75,389 fans, Connie, Bruce, and Lynne sat by running back Bill Mathis's father in the upper deck behind the Jets bench.

Three years earlier, the AFL and NFL—scheduled to merge in 1970—had arranged a postseason matchup between the champions of each league, a game eventually called Super Bowl I. The NFL team won the matchup that first year, and the next year, and the idea that an AFL team could finally beat them this time seemed like a Johnny Carson punch line. The NFL's best team that season was the Baltimore Colts, and fans watching NBC's Super Bowl pregame broadcast were reminded that, in the championship game the Colts played to reach the Super Bowl, they'd held their league's leading rusher to only 28 yards. Don Shula, their head coach, would end his career as the winningest coach in NFL history. The AFL champion Jets seemed no obstacle.

They brashly decided to show up anyway. From the swirling winds of Shea, they migrated to the sun-kissed shores of Florida for Super Bowl week. The Nicholas family arrived in waves: Connie and Bruce, with school as a consideration, were scheduled to fly down on Northeast Airlines after their parents. Connie spent the initial part of the trip calming Bruce, who was petrified about flying; by the time they deplaned, *she'd* become the nervous wreck. Chris had been unable to join them at all due to exams at Princeton, where friends teased him about the Jets' inevitable clobbering.

Then his father called.

"The players are really confident," he reported. "They don't think the Colts are so great."

Namath, who'd graduated from his slicked-over rookie haircut to the tousled, relaxed locks that foreshadowed the '70s, even publicly guaranteed a Jets win—which, among his lifetime of exploits, may have been the most shocking. "The Baltimore Colts are heavier favorites to win this Super Bowl game than [the NFL's] Green Bay was in 1967 and 1968," NBC's pregame intoned.

That afternoon inside the stadium, the scene began to take shape. On one sideline stood Baltimore's head coach, brown-haired Don Shula, a blue windbreaker over his dress shirt and tie; on the other, his silver-haired mentor Weeb Ewbank, who had coached the Jets since the Colts dismissed him in 1963.

On the Jets' sidelines, the personnel were focused as the game progressed. No one fooled around or cracked jokes, at least within Gerry Philbin's earshot. A missed field goal had stunted the Colts' offensive surge on their opening drive, while on the Jets' second possession, Namath threw a long, incomplete pass to Maynard. Connie learned later that was part of a decoy strategy. Maynard was playing hurt and couldn't capitalize on his superb speed. But if Namath threw his way occasionally, the Colts would think Maynard was fine and waste coverage on him.

The Colts, meanwhile, were having problems on both sides of the ball. Their quarterback Earl Morrall had enjoyed a standout year—in fact, the team had opted to start him over their storied signal caller Johnny Unitas, injured most of the season. But today, Morrall was having a bad outing at the worst possible moment. As the game progressed, the Jets defense would snatch away three of his passes. His defense was equally flustered, allowing the Jets' running back Matt Snell to find the end zone and push his team up 7–0 in the first half. As the second half ticked along, the Jets' Jim Turner kicked a field goal, then another.

Behind 13–0, with the clock counting down, the desperate Colts had to gamble.

They pulled Morrall and put Unitas in at quarterback.

The switch made even Philbin nervous. Though his body now bore the scars and aches of 14 years in professional football, Unitas was nevertheless a titan of the game, great enough and old enough that even the Jets roster revered him. He'd actually made Philbin cry once, when, in high school, the future defensive end watched his favorite team at the time, the New York Giants, lose to the Unitas-led Colts in the 1958 NFL championship. Weeb Ewbank knew all about Unitas, too; not only had he coached the Colts during that 1958 game, he'd given "Johnny U" his first real chance in professional football, after the Pittsburgh Steelers let him go before he'd ever thrown an NFL pass. Ewbank brought Unitas to Baltimore in 1956, which subsequently launched his Hall of Fame career.

Now Ewbank's Jets needed to hold against the quarterback he had plucked from obscurity 13 years ago.

In the stands, Connie's nerves grew taut. But she had faith, too—faith in the brilliance of Michaels's defensive acumen, which had served them so well for the better part of 60 minutes. It was a belief that, in general, Ewbank seemed to share. "Weeb Ewbank was famous for having really good system coaches, and I'd have to second that motion," says Bake. "I never saw Weeb overcoach a game."

First, the Jets added a field goal, which pushed the score to 16–0. But in a little over one quarter, Unitas threw for 110 yards with one interception. The Colts reached the end zone on a rushing play, making the score 16–7 as the clock ticked down in the fourth quarter. But it was the only time they'd find the scoreboard that day. As the game reached its dying minutes, Bake's mind finally began to relax.

We've got this thing won, he thought.

And they did. The Jets triumphed 16–7 in a victory that stunned the sports world. Michaels's defense had stopped a legend and created its own in the process. Jubilant, the players clad in green and white poured onto the field. Their win had changed not just their own franchise's standing, but the entire landscape of professional football. No one could say now the AFL didn't belong. As he ran off the field, Namath raised his index finger in a "No. 1" sign.

The celebrating followed. Connie snapped a picture of the diminutive Ewbank and the suave Namath—both in suits, and Namath sporting a Fu Manchu—holding a knife like newlyweds as they cut a cake during a celebration back at Shea Stadium. She witnessed Namath's glamorous entrance at a victory party with Suzy Storm on his arm, whom one of his teammates later called "the most beautiful blond[e] you ever saw in your life."[vii] At one event, a few players, including Namath, toasted Connie's uncle, presumably for the multiple knee operations he'd performed to keep them playing.[viii]

But the doctor wasn't the only Nicholas recipient of the quarterback's gratitude. In all his success, Namath never forgot the woman who gave him the St. Jude medal. He sent Julia Nicholas flowers every year on her birthday and wore the medal during games. One day, in the locker room, he realized it had been ripped off. Nearby was Bill Hampton, the Jets' equipment manager, who told his wife Dottie what had happened. She went out and found Namath a replacement. Even after his playing career ended, Namath continued to wear it, in part as a tribute to Dottie and Julia.

Her team finally belonged, but, as she graduated from high school that June, Connie was about to lose herself again. A while back, she'd started looking at colleges. Her mother thought it would be neat if she attended one of the revered "Seven Sister" schools, a collection of renowned, all-female East Coast institutions, but Connie's grades and SAT scores weren't high enough for admittance. Her sports prowess was virtually useless—female athletes generally weren't offered scholarships at the time, and some of the big colleges, like West Virginia University and University of Connecticut, still didn't have official women's basketball teams.

Even worse, she had no idea what she wanted to study. Career options for women post-college were narrow: teacher, nurse, social worker, or secretary were essentially the four fields they entered. At some point, though there had yet to be a female reporter in an NFL locker room, Connie asked *New York Post* journalist Paul Zimmerman, who'd become a famous *Sports Illustrated* columnist, to look at her sports writing.[ix] They'd met through her affiliation with the Jets, and he obligingly perused her articles for the Long Island Yacht Club newsletter, making notes on the margins of the typewritten pages. His mailed response that summer wasn't a ringing endorsement. "Your writing has a long way to go, but is not hopeless," his letter began.

By then, Connie had already settled her immediate future. Before transferring to Cornell, Lynne had gone to an all-girls junior college in New England and loved the experience. In the tiny town of Norton, Massachusetts, there was a small, all-women's school named Wheaton College that even had an official basketball team. Its greatest selling point was the beauty of the campus, which drew students in with its brick and marble buildings and classic, white New England chapel. Connie visited, lost her heart to the scenery, and applied. In December of 1968, she got an acceptance letter: she'd be attending Wheaton the following autumn.

But the decision foretold change, and some of the most difficult had to do with football. The school was too far away for frequent visits home, which meant, for the first time in half a decade, she'd be absent on autumn Sundays at Shea and would miss all the casual, social interactions with the Jets. In the off-season, some of the players assembled a basketball squad to play in exhibition games against various organizations—police groups, men's associations, sometimes the faculty of a school. It was a way for the players to earn a few needed bucks—they normally got around $50 apiece for a basketball game—and also served as a fundraiser for the organizations they battled against. Equipment manager Bill Hampton was often the point person for the endeavor. He'd contact the players, arrange pickup locations for them to carpool to the venue, and bring their green-and-white basketball uniforms to the game site. The Nicholas family usually came to cheer the team on, a gesture of support not lost on the players. "We'd look up, and here we are, seven or eight guys who played basketball in the off-season to make a few extra dollars, and who would you see in the stands but Connie and her father and her mother," says Philbin. "That's the kind of great fans they were, they not only were fans during the season."

During the off-season that followed Super Bowl III, the Jets played a game against faculty and alumni of Babylon High School, and Connie got to escort the team into the gymnasium. It would be hard to top the exhilaration she felt in that moment as others looked on while she walked with the reigning Super Bowl champs into the four walls of her high school kingdom and basked in their glow.[1] Following the game, her parents hosted a gathering back at the Nicholas house.

Bereft of a prom experience—she wasn't asked—the party served as one of her most vivid high school memories, likely because Bake came and borrowed her acoustic guitar to entertain the group. Sauer perched nearby, accompanying him on the electric guitar. The chords reverberated through the Nicholas porch, mixing with laughter and the sound of dishes clinking. Connie, her teenage heart fluttering, sat at the musicians' feet, capturing the music on her reel-to-reel tape recorder. The thin strip of tape went round and round, a silent chronicler of history. It caught Sauer's wife, Janet, wandering aimlessly through part of "Hey

---

[1] Her brother, Chris, actually took part in the game; he played for Babylon as an alum of the school.

Jude," then trying another tune before Bake bailed her out; it caught Michael Keeshan trying in vain to attract Connie's attention. Reddish-haired, freckled Michael was the son of neighbor Bob Keeshan, better known as the TV celebrity Captain Kangaroo, and so popular at the time that Jets running back Emerson Boozer was excited to meet *him*. When Michael and Connie were younger, they'd arranged to marry each other, but she backed out of the deal when he topped out several inches shorter than she. Tonight, despite his best efforts, she refused to be distracted from the Texas crooner. At one point, Michael even unplugged her recorder; she plugged it back in.

Round and round, the strip of tape had danced that evening:

Her grandmother Mimi, curious to know the names of the guitar chords: *What are the strings on that, Mr. Sauer?*

Sauer: *Steel.*

Bake, gaily trying to toss the rest of "Cotton Fields Back Home" to his fellow guitarist: *Take it, George!*

Sauer: *I don't know it, man.*

Connie kept the recording long after the party ended. In later years, whenever she listened, the scene sprang to life again—the laughter, the people, the music, her delight at being surrounded by those dearest to her, Bake's winsome voice, all the happy refrain of childhood she never wanted to end.

Yet that fall, she packed her bags, said goodbye to life with the Jets, and headed north to New England.

Part II: Making History

She's the kind of a girl that would probably be a success in any endeavor she attempted.

— CHARLEY WINNER
FORMER HEAD COACH
NEW YORK JETS

CHAPTER 8

Of Sororities and a Star Quarterback

Wheaton College, spring, 1970.

The school was resplendent in its New England beauty. On the older section of campus—the area not infested with '70s-style architecture—trees surrounded a picturesque green known as the dimple, which sloped slightly inward on all sides. From the dining hall, had she cared to look, Connie could have watched the ducks paddling around the pond as she ate lunch. The pond itself was magnificent. Its glassy surface rippled when caressed by the wind, and a small, arched footbridge extending across offered a picturesque walk from the dining hall to several main buildings on campus.

And yet, she was miserable.

The Vietnam War had turned colleges into a cauldron of political sentiment. That May, students angry over President Nixon's military policies and the death of four Kent State protestors shut down 200 campuses nationwide.[i] In a stunning move, Nixon's secretary of the interior, Walter J. Hickel, had written to the president, indirectly chastising his leadership, and the letter had somehow leaked to the press: "About 200 years ago there was emerging a great nation in the British Empire, and it found itself with a colony in violent protest by its youth—men such as Patrick Henry, Thomas Jefferson, Madison and Monroe, to name a few," Hickel had penned (his own son was set to join protestors on a San Francisco campus the following day but maintained his father had thought of the letter sans his son's influence).[ii] Dr. Cal was so enraged by Hickel's statements that he wrote a response in the local Babylon newspaper: "What about listening to my two college children, who happen to disagree with you about the protestors?" he flared. "You want to listen to the violent protestors but you don't want to listen to people who want to go to class."[iii]

In fact, it hadn't taken Connie long to realize her political leanings were at odds with Wheaton's progressive style. Feeling isolated, she began writing to prominent conservative thinker William F. Buckley, who invited her to watch a taping of his show, *Firing Line*, in New York. But on campus—where friendships dissolved over political disagreements—the political talk drove her crazy. In addition, the era of sex, drugs, and rock 'n' roll was beginning to permeate institutions of higher learning, and Wheaton's student body enthusiastically embraced the trend. Connie, aligning more with the morals and sentiment of her parents' generation, again found herself in the minority.

Fortunately, just as in high school, she still found ways to get along with everybody. Connie was never afraid to be fun—she'd traipse down to the underutilized dorm kitchen, bake brownies, and guilelessly distribute them to her dorm mates, even the rock 'n' rollers who danced to a more adventuresome moral code. But some of the trends just didn't make sense to her. Everyone was smoking pot, which gave them the munchies, and why would someone want that? She already had enough trouble with her weight. In fact, by the time she returned home at the end of her first year, she'd gained 10 pounds.

This was a crisis. She went to her dad for help; since diet pills containing speed were legal at the time, Dr. Cal prescribed some for her. The pills worked, and her weight dropped.

But back at school, she floundered. Still undecided on a career, she'd kept taking religion classes because she adored the professor, white-haired Dr. Martin. Majoring in religion, however, seemed pointless—one thing she didn't want to be was a nun.

She hadn't completely abandoned her sportswriting idea. She wrote to George Sauer's dad, George Sauer Sr., about it freshman year and included some draft talk in her letter. The elder Sauer had recently been hired as the Boston Patriots' general manager, and his response came back that February on official team letterhead:

Dear Connie,

I'm terribly embarrassed to be so late in acknowledging your recent letter and the reason I can give is that we have been extremely busy trying to sign our Draftees and meeting and worrying about a stadium in Boston for the 1970 season.

Connie, it would please me a great deal to recommend you as a Sportswriter. With your ability, desire, and knowledge in the field of sports, I know you will be outstanding.

Burnett of Arkansas and Poppe of Missouri are Juniors and will not be eligible for the draft until after the 1970 football season.

I will look forward to hearing from you soon. In the meantime, please relay my best wishes to your Mother and Dad.

Sincerely,

George Sauer (Sr.)

This was encouraging, but as she had no idea where to go from there, the topic soon dropped.

She'd proudly carried on her Jets fandom at Wheaton. On the walls of her dorm room, along with images of William F. Buckley and singer Glen Campbell, she hung two gigantic posters of George Sauer and Joe Namath. She even spurred one of her roommates, Cynthia, to eventually start watching football. Cynthia's dad had played semi-pro ball, yet she'd remained stoically disinterested in football growing up. But when Connie began sharing stories about the team, Cynthia found herself growing interested in the people. One day, a group of ladies came to visit Connie at the dorms, and Mrs. Emerson Boozer, the wife of Jets running back Emerson Boozer, was with them. Cynthia, standing there in her bathrobe, soaked in the scene. The players had started out as mere posters on a wall. But living in Connie's orbit, they came alive.

Cynthia's friendship, in fact, was one of the best things about Wheaton. The girls had met Connie's freshman year, when Cynthia lived in the dorm room next door. Cynthia, although not wild, was certainly liberal (in fact, they were dubbed "Miss Liberal" and "Miss Conservative"), but considered Connie one of the most non-judgmental people she knew. And Connie was far from a stick in the mud; sometimes, she and Cynthia listened to music in the dorm, and when they blared the Rolling Stones' smash "Honky Tonk Woman," on the record player, Connie turned into a wild, dancing machine, moving crazily around the room.

But secretly, she was still miserable.

Part of it was homesickness. She missed going to her brothers' sporting events. Back home, there were always boys' games to attend as well as girls'—in fact, the Nicholas family had often attended football games at Babylon High even without a son or brother on the sidelines. Here, there was no such outlet. She didn't fit in interest-wise or ideologically; just when she was supposed to be finding herself, she felt completely lost. Even playing basketball couldn't lift her spirits. The athletic community on Wheaton's campus was low-key—the student body had scant interest in attending the games or supporting the teams on campus. Connie's high school career had carried more significance. Sometimes, her heart aching for home, she hid in the closet of her dorm room and cried.

But the biggest problem was the boys.

There were few of these fascinating creatures floating around campus, except a handful that came as part of an exchange program with a few other schools. But in absentia, they exerted even more power. On weekends, Wheaton emptied as the girls flocked to visit their boyfriends' schools. Connie, as usual, didn't have a boyfriend, which meant she was left behind on a dull, mostly deserted campus.

She tried to fix the problem. Wheaton, as an all-girls school, sponsored mixers where their students traveled to boys' schools for social events, and Connie decided to attend. The Wheaton girls rode over together, and, on reaching their destination, filed off the bus and walked into a big room, where the event suddenly turned into a gauntlet: as each girl entered, a boy, if he felt interested, walked up and picked her to be his date for the evening. When Connie walked in, no one came up, leaving her alone in a crowd of couples. She spent most of the evening embarrassed and in anguish, for once too insecure to even walk around and attempt conversation.

Still, she didn't give up. Chris volunteered to set her up with a hockey player at Princeton if she'd return the favor with a particular friend at Wheaton. She obliged, but while her brother and friend had a fabulous time, Connie and her date—despite the great sports conversation—had no spark. A separate blind date involved a trip to Boston for an outing with three other couples. At first, she and her date strolled along the sidewalk in Boston, holding hands, until a wave of people moving the opposite direction forced them to break their hold. When Connie made it through to the other side, she looked around. The rest of the group was there, but her date had vanished. Using the crowd as cover, he'd slipped away, deserting her. She tried not to make a big deal of it in front of the group as they continued on—less one person—but there was nowhere to hide, step after agonizing step, as she burned with embarrassment, the other couples witnessing her shame.

Finally, she'd had enough. When she went home for Christmas during her sophomore year, she told her parents she wanted to transfer; when they asked why, she explained that, since Wheaton was a liberal arts school, there was nothing study-wise that interested her as a major. They agreed, and she set about applying to other schools. This time, she went in the opposite direction: Pennsylvania State University, the University of Connecticut, and The Ohio State University, all big, state schools. Two Jets players, Matt Snell and Dave Foley, had told her about OSU, where they'd played football under the school's legendary coach, Woody Hayes. In the end, Penn and UConn seemed disinclined to accept students from out of state, but OSU proved more welcoming. The school admitted her, and when the autumn of 1971 rolled around, it found her bound for Columbus, Ohio, ready for a new adventure.

But there had been one other change before she left Wheaton. Connie went to her father and asked if she could get a nose job. She just couldn't be "Captain Hook" anymore, she explained.

Dr. Cal was concerned.

"After you have one thing done, are you going to want a million other things done?" he asked. "Are you ever going to be happy with yourself?"

Connie reassured him this was her only quibble. At that point, they didn't know to go to a plastic surgeon for the procedure—not even Dr. Cal, with all his medical knowledge—and so Connie went to an ear, nose and throat physician instead. The doctor ended up botching the job, and Connie couldn't help but feel that, while better than before, her nose still left something to be desired.

After Wheaton, Ohio State was a breath of fresh air.

The ideological tension was still there—OSU, with its massive student body, was not immune to the culture fomented by the war or the new, freewheeling lifestyle Connie had encountered at Wheaton. But here, there were contravening forces. One such entity was Greek life, whose popularity had taken a hit because it represented structure and tradition at a time when people sought to live outside such things. The '70s were about living life unfettered, and Greek organizations had *rules*. But Connie loved tradition, and she'd never had trouble following rules. Someone invited her to rush, and she accepted, even though she had no idea what rushing was. Each sorority on campus, she soon realized, had a different persona—cheerleaders, for example, generally pledged Pi Phi or Delta Delta Delta. She discovered the Zeta Tau Alphas, while not the glamorous, cheerleader types, proved a wonderful, diverse group of girls. She rushed, was invited to join Zeta, and moved into the sorority house her second year on campus.

But, even better, Ohio State had football—big, vibrant, thriving college football. At the time, they were embroiled in what became known as the Ten Year War with the University of Michigan—a veritable blood feud that stoked one of the biggest, fiercest rivalries in college football. On Ohio State's campus, the word "Michigan" was essentially forbidden; students replaced it with the less vulgar phrase, "The State Up North." They did the reverse to Michigan's fight song, swapping its lyrics with crass language.

Regardless, the environment was a football fanatic's dream. Connie thrilled, on game days, to walk to St. John Arena and hear the marching band fire up the crowd before heading to the football stadium. And then, to be back watching football again—surrounded by over 80,000 people—all cheering, screaming deliriously, as the Buckeyes battled that week's opponent! Led by their legendary head coach, Woody Hayes, Ohio State would string together two of four consecutive Rose Bowl appearances while she was at the school. Hayes was a fascinating mix of strength and emotion. He was tough on his players and tough on his coaches, consumed with passion for his sport. The media would see his fiery—and ultimately, his worst—side, when, in the late '70s, that passion got the better of him and he punched an opposing team's player near the Ohio State sidelines. Apathy was Hayes's mortal enemy.

"Boys," he told his players once, "I don't want you on the football field if you're going to show any signs of apathy. *Apathy*," he repeated, writing it up on the chalkboard, the young men's eyes glued to his every move. "Avoid it like the plague. It's the damndest thing in the world, and you'll run into these guys this fall on the campus"—here Hayes dropped his tone, slowing his speech to a lazy cadence—"'*Why play football? You work too hard. Why do that? Come on and have a joint with me.*'"

The players burst out laughing.

"He'll sit there and look at his shoe for an hour," continued Hayes, warming to his subject. "You think I'm kidding you? I'm not kidding you, am I?" The players assented. "And those people are apathetic as hell, and they're going *NOWHERE*. And there are a hell of a lot of people, and they take a lot of people with them, fellas. They take a lot of people with them. 'Cause we all have a tendency to be lazy. And I don't know whether it's body chemistry, or mind, or whether it's a combination. It has to be a little bit of both. We all have a tendency to ease off at times. That's why you need good teachers and good coaches to push you a little bit. We *all* have to be pushed. The fact I'm a football coach—it's a competitive thing. I despise for people to beat us. That's why, when I get good football players, I'm not going to let someone else beat us. 'Cause I'm cheating myself and I'm cheating my players if we don't get the best out of them."[iv]

But George Hill, who coached the Ohio State defense, knew there was also a side to Hayes the media rarely saw—a man of compassion and character, the kind that made Hill insist he had no better friend in the world than Woody Hayes. The white-haired head coach with the glasses and baseball cap became like a father to many of the players who entered his program from tough backgrounds. More than anything, Hayes wanted his players to graduate college, and for those who didn't, he pestered them until they came back to school and finished their degree.

Hayes's commitment to students' education, Hill discovered, extended beyond the football program. One afternoon, the head coach invited Hill to lunch, and the two trekked across campus to the faculty club, where a young co-ed waited on their table.

"Coach, this'll be the last time I'm going to see you for a while," she told Hayes. "I'm going to have to drop out of school and go to work, come back."

"How many quarters do you have to go?" he asked.

"I have two quarters," she answered, "but I don't have any more money. I'm going to have to drop out."

"Working here at the faculty room, you get your meals and so for free, don't you?" Hayes queried.

"Yeah," she confirmed.

"You can't drop out of school now," he insisted.

"I'm just going to have to," she said.

But Hayes wouldn't let the matter rest.

"You come over to see me tomorrow morning in my office at nine o'clock," he said.

The next morning, she arrived promptly at Hayes's office. Hill, who had the next office over, saw her leave about 45 minutes later and noticed she was crying.

He walked over to Hayes.

"Coach, is she okay?" Hill asked.

"Oh yes, she's doing fine," Hayes said. "I told her I was going to take care of her fees and tuition for the next two quarters so she could graduate." The coach explained she'd objected that she couldn't pay him back. Hayes had merely responded, "Well, someday in the future, somebody's going to need some help. You remember that, and you pay that forward."

Then he told Hill an even more remarkable story. When he won the national championship in 1954, the alumni bought him a Cadillac. He told the alumni to take the car back; he didn't want *any* gift like that (he wasn't a Cadillac kind of guy, anyway—he drove Fords). They responded they couldn't—people from all over the state had donated to buy the car. So Hayes told them instead to take the money and put it in the bank, declaring it would never be spent on himself or his family. In 1957, the pattern repeated: he won the national championship, the alumni bought him the car, and Hayes again objected.

"That money went in the bank," he told Hill. "Not one penny of it was ever spent on anybody in the Hayes family. But that's paid the fees and tuitions of 73 students here at Ohio State."

Such was Woody Hayes: passionate, determined, unafraid to think for himself, a coaching legend.

Connie, bursting with football fervor, decided she had to meet him. She possessed a knack for meeting generally inaccessible people; as a kid, she'd once stood at a baseball game trying to collect players' autographs as everyone hollered at the athletes to come over. They refused, but went right to Connie when she called out. Chris, waiting there with her, realized it was because she'd politely include "Mr." before a player's last name when she called to them. Another time, a ring of bodyguards was protecting William F. Buckley's brother, Jim—who won a U.S. Senate seat in 1970—at a Jets game. Chris glanced over at one point and was stunned when he saw the person who'd finagled a way through the protection detail and now sat talking to Mr. Buckley was his sister. Connie, however, was generally oblivious to her gift; most of the time, she had no idea she was doing anything special.

At Ohio State, there was a particular dining hall where the football team ate its meals. One day, Connie hung around outside the building till Hayes emerged; then, she boldly approached and introduced herself. Thus waylaid, the fiery football coach did an amazing thing—he smiled. In fact, he couldn't have been nicer. They chatted cordially, and Connie walked away thrilled. After that, whenever she saw him, they struck up a conversation. She mentioned her father and uncle were the team doctors for the Jets. They talked about Ohio State linebacker Randy Gradishar's knees (he had to go to New York for a fitting of the same type of brace her Uncle Jim helped invent for Joe Namath),[v] the Jets, and life in general. During one conversation, Hayes offered, "Come over to my office anytime, and let's talk football."

So she went over to his office and talked more football, but also found herself pouring her heart out to the coaching legend.

"I'm majoring in home ec education and dietetics, but I love football," she confessed. "And I don't know what to do. I think I'm going to teach, and then maybe coach girls' basketball after school."

"Well, you've got to keep after your passion, whatever it is," Hayes encouraged. "Just keep doing what you're doing, and something's going to happen."

And then, he said something extraordinary:

"In the meantime, you come to every practice at Ohio State. Even if it's closed to everybody else—*you come.*"

It was a jaw-dropping offer. Many people weren't welcome to Ohio State football practices—including some scouts when practices were closed.[1] But Hayes, sometimes viewed as being too tyrannical, had just thrown open the doors of one of the country's most prestigious college football programs to a fresh-faced, twenty-something *girl* he barely knew. A lot of coaches wouldn't have done it. But Hayes seemed to sense that, in their deep, abiding love of the game, the white-haired coach and the exuberant young woman were two of a kind.

Connie was elated. The tutorials she'd enjoyed under Paul Albert now graduated to the vast expanse of the Ohio State football stadium, where she walked over each day after classes finished to observe practice.

---

[1] "There was a closed practice, and then there was a Michigan practice," Hill says. "Nobody got into those."

During the season, she kept a respectful distance, but in spring practice, she drew close to observe the action. She wanted to know everything, down to why a coach had run a certain drill. Careful not to bother the coaches during practice, she stored her questions for afterwards or before practice began. Sometimes, she even went to their offices to chat between classes. It was impossible *not* to notice her, George Hill felt—she was always around, full of life and full of football. He appreciated that trait in a woman; his own wife was so knowledgeable about the game that Hill, who later joined an NFL coaching staff, realized the stats she kept on yellow legal pads were better than ones they had in the NFL. Several of the coaches' wives had little interest in the sport itself, but Mrs. George Hill, née Cloyed Ray, was different. She'd met her husband at the Philadelphia naval hospital, when she was a navy nurse lieutenant J. G. and he was a seaman first-class. The moment she walked into the room, dressed in her white uniform, with the nurse's cap perched on her head, Hill took notice. He asked her out multiple times, but, since she was an officer and he was enlisted, any fraternization between the two was forbidden. When his rejection count neared double digits, Hill, figuring she was bent on following the rules, was about to give up. Then, one day, another young nurse came by and queried if he ever planned to ask Miss Ray out again.

"I don't think so," he confessed. "Every time I've asked her to do something, she's always turned me down."

"You know what," the nurse hinted, "you ought to rethink that."

Hill went back to his barracks and sat down on his bunk.

Those girls must be talking, he realized.

A few days later, he ran into Cloyed Ray again. He made another attempt.

"Miss Ray," he ventured, "would you like to go to the movie?"

This time, he got the response he'd been waiting for.

Now, when he heard Connie discuss football, he could relate to a young woman so passionate about understanding the sport, thanks to his wife.

He also observed the young co-ed chatting with the scouts who came to Ohio State to report on players (one of Hill's responsibilities was serving as a liaison between the scouts and the school's coaching staff). Scouting visits followed a similar pattern: the school provided the scouts with a projector and whatever 16mm film of games they requested so that they could watch and take notes on how certain players performed. When the coaching staff had a spare minute, the scouts stopped by to chat, trying to glean more about an individual player's personality. Several asked specifically about work and study habits: what kind of student the player was, if they worked at their academics, how committed they were to the game of football, whether the coaches felt they could play at the NFL level. The scouts also took in a practice at the stadium so they could observe the players in person. There, Connie, outgoing and eager to learn, fell into the habit of talking with them.

Those conversations, perhaps, were spurred by a self-revelation she'd had one day for a class assignment. She and her peers were instructed to compose a brief essay describing their ideal day five years in the future—consideration could be given to how they would look, where they might be, and who would be in their life. Taking her pen in hand, Connie wrote a frank, honest revelation of the dreams nearest her 20-year-old heart:

> *I will be 25 years old, hopefully looking much as I do now. I will be married (almost 6 months) to a man that will be the dominant one, steady job, stable person, also want a family and loves sports. If he wants me to stay at home and not work, I would gladly do so. If not, I will be either teaching home economics in junior high and coaching girls' basketball and softball after school, or a possibility of secretary, scout, or PR for a sports team. Whichever, it will be with people—lots of them.*

Had the epistle ever circulated among some of her progressive peers, her traditional leanings would likely have scandalized. In reality, she was proving more feminist than many dared dream. The idea of a woman scout in the NFL—which she'd hinted at so casually in her musings—was borderline *revolutionary*. The profession was a veritable men's club, a quiet, unassuming bastion of the good old boys' network. But Connie never thought of them as enemies to her ambitions—some of her greatest mentors and encouragers had been men, going back to Paul Albert and Walt Michaels. Sitting there, pen in hand, an inviting sheet of paper before her, the desire had poured out. Perhaps it was the first time she'd really known her own heart.

At the sorority house, meanwhile, the upcoming officer elections were causing her angst. A few of the girls had asked her to run for chapter president. Technically, the rules stated one had to be a member of ZTA for a certain length of time before becoming president, a requirement Connie had not yet met. But her sorority sisters were so fond of her that they petitioned the national headquarters for an exception. She wasn't running unopposed, however—a young woman named Nancy Ashton had also filed for the position. While visiting with her grandparents, who'd come to Columbus to see her, Connie threw herself on the hotel bed in a fit of youthful anxiety.

"I'm just a failure," she declared.

But Dziadzie, as usual, was reassuring.

"No," he comforted her. "You're going to be just fine."

He was right. She won the election and the chapter also received the needed dispensation from headquarters. The energetic new president, who'd been a social misfit at Wheaton, now led her sorority sisters as they marched through the house, belting out the school's fight song, before joining the red-clad masses to hear the band play before football games.

Dr. Cal and Lynne also traveled to Columbus for a few of the games. Her first semester, when Ohio State played Colorado, Connie and her father argued about Colorado prospect Cliff Branch, whose overall performance—despite a key punt return for a touchdown—failed to impress the doctor. Connie, however, insisted she saw something there; she felt vindicated when he was drafted by the Oakland Raiders at the end of the season and eventually won three Super Bowls. The Nicholas family had a habit of arguing over players—she took on her Uncle Jim over Ohio State linebacker Randy Gradishar when he suggested Gradishar wouldn't last in the NFL, but Connie was convinced he would thrive. Dr. Jim often teased and tested her knowledge of the game and personnel; he once told his son, Philip, that she had unerring instinct when it came to observing talent.

Another weekend, she took her parents to the Jai Lai restaurant in Columbus, which Woody Hayes often patronized. Hayes was there that day and spent a long time chatting with her father. Later, he sent the doctor a note, with a cordial opening line inviting him to attend practice "any time you visit campus." Dr. Cal—generally the least assuming of men—thought this must be due to his position with the Jets and Hayes's friendship with Weeb Ewbank.

But the next sentence made it very clear to whom he owed the honor: should the doctor attend practice, Hayes wrote, "[y]ou will have to be accompanied by your daughter."

Dr. Cal, sensing the coach would ultimately prefer he *didn't* come, decided he'd refrain from imposing on Connie. He felt afterwards the coach appreciated his awareness, for Hayes remained very gracious to him—away from the practice field.

The vast, horseshoe-shaped structure, with its carpet of green, was by far his daughter's favorite classroom at Ohio State, although she was doing well enough as a home economics education and dietetics major by the end of her first year that she was eligible to join the home economics honors program the following August. She hit a roadblock with her major one semester when she was assigned a sewing project in one of her classes. Connie hated sewing, or what she knew of it, since she'd never actually learned—her grandmother Mimi had made most of her granddaughter's clothes growing up. Nor did Connie feel like learning now; going to football practice sounded much more appealing. A few sorority sisters rescued her by offering to help out with the project; Connie left them sewing while she trekked happily off to the stadium.

The entire house drew inspiration from her football obsession. Knowing her relationship with the Jets, the girls asked Connie if Joe Namath would be willing to serve as the chapter's unofficial "little brother," a figurehead role with an honorary title and no obligations. They had a green shirt with "ZTA" in white lettering printed, and Connie mailed it off to Namath with the request. Namath, despite his stratospheric celebrity, good-naturedly obliged; he even posed in the shirt so that Connie could snap a picture, then wore it again when he and the Jets' new head coach, Charley Winner, stood together, holding a football, as a beat reporter for the *Daily News* snapped a photograph.

She also took one of her college friends, Pat Pinkham, to meet the quarterback when the two girls were visiting Julia Nicholas at her new home in Florida during spring break. Namath had an offseason apartment not far away, and he graciously let the two unannounced visitors in when they stopped by to say hello. He lounged comfortably in a straight-backed chair in the corner, a newspaper on the floor beside him, while Connie and Pat sat together on a nearby couch. Connie felt so shy that she just talked football the whole time. Not nearly as glamorous—and far more distressing—were the several pounds she gained on the trip from her grandmother's rich cooking.

At school, her eating habits had grown extreme. Having lost so much weight at Wheaton, she now developed an eating disorder trying to keep it off.[2] On Sundays, she binged, consuming five ice cream sundaes, ten sandwiches, spaghetti, or other assortments of calorie-laden foods, which resulted in a three to four-pound weight gain. Then, on Mondays and Tuesdays, she ate only a bagel. The weight vanished. On Wednesdays, the pattern repeated—she gorged again, then spent Thursday through Saturday losing the weight. But people had begun to make flattering comments about her figure, so she grasped desperately at this one shred of confidence. Convinced a boy would

[2] She'd quit taking the speed pills while still at Wheaton as soon as she'd lost the original weight.

only love her for her body, it was her own eyes that viewed her in the harshest light.

And there was still heartache. The sorority held a beautiful ceremony known as a lavalier whenever one of their own got engaged: all the girls gathered in a circle, and a lighted candle was passed around while they sang, until it came to the engaged girl, who blew it out. It was exciting and joyful, but a girl who hadn't had one of those ceremonies by the time she graduated evoked sympathy. Connie appeared nowhere close—she had only gone on what she considered her first "real" date when she was 21, and even then hadn't been overly interested in the guy, but for the first time, a boy was actually *nice* and treated her well. They went out a few times, although Connie had to admit there was no spark.

Then, one weekend while at a Young Republicans convention, she met a handsome visiting student named Denny from Bowling Green University. Connie was smitten, and he seemed interested, too—he soon invited her to his home in Cleveland, where she also met his mother and father, who'd emigrated from Hungary. Connie thought they were lovely people. But their son crushed any hope she had of a future with him as they talked during her stay. "I told other girls," he revealed, "that I wish they could have your heart, and I wish you could have their looks." Connie never forgot his remark—it stung and stirred all the insecurities that had taken root in her soul. She had been told that she was not enough; that her character and heart were insufficient to overcome someone's opinion of how she should look. It felt like the opposite of a fairy tale. The two stayed in touch for a while, but romance had vanished.

But now, at least—unlike Wheaton—there were other avenues buoying her confidence. In the spring of her junior year, she received a letter from Mike Holovak, a scout for the Jets during the '72 season before being named offensive backs coach the following year. Holovak was a tall, thin man, with eyes that at first seemed almost too kind for football, until one looked at his work and realized those same eyes were piercing in their evaluation of talent. Connie had talked with him on her last visit home, and in April of 1973, he thought to send her a scouting report of players he'd been evaluating:

> *Dear Connie,*
>
> *Just returned from my spring practice scouting tour and since I know of no one with a deeper interest than yourself, I thought an immediate report should be sent along. No question but that good old Ohio State would rank up near the top of my list this coming season, but I did take in two schools that would make it quite interesting for the Buckeyes, both as a team and as a source for pro talent, namely the University of Colorado and Nebraska. The people at Boulder are still smiling over their victory at Columbus not too very long ago.*
>
> *A quick résumé of some top one[s]—Colorado has a tight end Cain, and a [running back] named Matthews who look very good at*

this writing. Also a great big defensive lineman named Sens, and a wide receiver Keyworth. They also have five or six others who will be drafted but maybe not as high choices as the first mentioned.

At Nebraska, they have a defensive lineman named John Dutton who is big and very quick. It would make for an interesting afternoon if he were to play vs. your John Hicks. They also have an offensive lineman who looks good ... plus a half dozen others who will be drafted a bit later.

Those are the top ones I see and the two top teams. Hope you enjoy the report. Enjoyed chatting with you on your last visit. Sure do enjoy chatting with your Dad. Like yourself, he is so enthusiastic. Have a nice spring and a pleasant summer.

Regards,

Mike Holovak

Had Connie been able to see the future, she would have found Holovak's assessment notably accurate; the following draft, Dutton was taken fifth overall by the Colts (and lasted 14 seasons in the league), with exactly half a dozen other Nebraska players drafted in the fourth round or later, just as Holovak projected. Colorado's Matthews and Cain also went in the first round, although Sens and Keyworth were taken much later. There were six other players taken out of Colorado that draft—again, exactly as Holovak predicted, though the rounds differed slightly. Of the players Holovak named as having impressed him, Sens proved the only bust in the NFL.

She had, over several years, built a network of people whose instincts and knowledge had given her an extraordinary foundation to understand the game. From the moment she stepped into Paul Albert's office as a 12-year-old girl, she had been learning—at each new turn, she had chased down every lead, every conversation, every morsel of insight within reach to better understand the sport she loved. But now, as she neared graduation, no place appeared to exist where she could put that hard-earned knowledge to use. Title IX, passed in 1972, had changed the landscape of collegiate and high school sports for women forever, but there was no such force at work in pro sports administration, virtually no trailblazers for her to look to. For a girl who loved football, the road essentially began and ended with fandom.[vi]

Pondering her next step, Connie called the Ohio State football office and reached Hayes's secretary. She asked if she could speak with the coach about somehow breaking into the sports world. The secretary quickly set up an appointment with Hayes at the practice field, and Connie met him there. The players were arriving for practice, and a few wandered by, but Hayes gave the young student his undivided attention. They talked about graduate school in a sports-related field. They discussed whether she wanted sports to become her life, or remain a hobby. Hayes promised to assist any way he could. They talked for 45 minutes.

In the end, he couldn't offer a solution, but by the time she walked away, he'd given her something much more: the confidence to follow her passion. She would keep striving to find her place in sports, even if she couldn't yet explain how, or where. Someway, it would all work out.

CHAPTER 9

Sink—or Swim

But when Connie returned to Babylon after graduation in June 1974, her sports dreams appeared no closer to being realized. The most natural starting point, the Jets, wasn't a plausible option—their head coach, Charley Winner, had only recently replaced his father-in-law, Weeb Ewbank, in the job, and Connie knew the decision had prompted whispers of nepotism against the franchise. With a father and uncle already on staff, her own cause seemed hopeless.

Fat chance of working for them, she thought.

There were teaching jobs available, however, so Connie opted to start out teaching and coaching, a combination that had merited honorable mention in her "ideal future day" musings (the husband, much like the sports career, had also failed to materialize so far).[i] Babylon High, her former high school, offered her a job; she figured they'd have no trouble letting her coach as well.

She also returned to the Long Island Yacht Club (LIYC), where she'd lifeguarded the previous summer, as pool director and head swim coach for the season. As always, open to self-improvement and unthreatened by constructive input, she worked together with one of the swimmers, a standout named Rob Russell (it was his mother who, along with Lynne, had dressed in swim team colors during meets), figuring out the best positioning and matchups to give the LIYC team an advantage. Connie proved an energetic coach—though competitive, she focused on positive reinforcement, a contrast, perhaps, to many of the male coaches at the time. She looked different, too, with her long brown hair in curls and slender, long, tanned legs. "That was the first person I remember [thinking], 'Oh, she had nice legs,'" a young swimmer at the club admitted later. "From then on, I've been a leg man." But the girl with the knockout pins also proved an excellent instructor—the team finished that season as undefeated champions.

The kids found there were advantages, too, to having a coach whose dad was a doctor for the New York Jets. If Dr. Cal knew Joe Namath was coming to his home office, the doctor always made sure to mention it to Connie, who allowed the swimmers to make the short walk up the street and sit quietly in the grass along the Nicholas driveway so they could see Namath.

One time, she'd called Rob, who lived just a block and a half away, with a valuable tip.

"Don't tell anybody," she cautioned, "but Joe Namath is getting his physical at my father's office. Get over here as soon as you can."

That was all Rob needed to hear. He hopped on his bike, zipped over to the Nicholas house, and rang the bell. The door opened—but there was no Connie greeting him at the doorway. Lynne Nicholas stood there, assessing the situation.

"Now, what are you doing here right now?" she asked knowingly, before relenting. "Alright. Get in there and sit up on the couch."

Rob went inside and sat down, discovering quickly he wasn't the only one who'd been forewarned of the quarterback's visit—about half a dozen autograph hopefuls were lined up on the couch with him, waiting for Namath. Their devotion was ultimately rewarded: when the broad-shouldered quarterback emerged, he signed footballs for all of them.

Even knowing an insider like Connie, however, never guaranteed such opportunities. The doctor's daughter, conscious of the demands on Namath's time, tried to be careful what she asked of him. Fortunately, Namath was magnanimous—he appeared not to take his fans' attention for granted, despite their omnipresence. Even after the quarterback retired, the team's public relations director Frank Ramos would be out with him at a restaurant in New York when he'd hear someone say, "Isn't that Joe Namath?" Well-dressed, older patrons came *back* into the restaurant to gawk at him. One gentleman, explaining that he was an ambassador to the U. N., approached and asked for a picture. Namath got up in the middle of dinner to pose for it.

"Joe, you must hear those people when they're saying, 'That's Joe Namath,'" Ramos observed. "You had to have heard those people."

"Yeah," Namath responded. "And I hope it never stops."

There was also one glorious time when Connie got to ride with him in his open-top convertible from Babylon to the nearby town of West Islip.[ii] Connie's beloved Dziadzie had passed away while she was still at OSU, and Mimi was now selling the couple's house; Namath, visiting with the Nicholas family after a stop at Dr. Cal's office, expressed interest. Connie agreed to show him the property. She climbed into Namath's convertible and rode with him down the main streets of Babylon, wishing the whole world could see her. Too soon, they were at West Islip, and she was showing Namath around her grandmother's place, a white house on land bordering the water. Namath didn't end up purchasing the property, but it was still a thrilling memory, both for Connie and the young boy from the LIYC swim team who lived across the street and still recalled, years later, the day a convertible pulled into his neighbor's driveway and *Joe Namath*, accompanied by a very excited swim coach, stepped out.

For Connie, it was thrilling to be back, immersed in the world of the Jets. Before her senior year of high school, the team had finally moved their summer training away from Peekskill, and now she could observe practice at their new location at Hofstra University in Hempstead, New York, just 25 minutes away.[iii] Her mother also threw a surprise 50th birthday brunch for Dr. Cal that summer at a local country club, and Jets personnel turned out in force for the doctor's fete. The Boozers were there, Dottie and Bill Hampton, Ralph Baker, the team's traveling secretary John Free, and his wife, Ruth. Even Paul Albert and his wife, Betty, attended. The men wore suits—some of them featuring the plaid patterns that had become popular; the women primarily donned skirts or nice dresses.

Connie, already tanned from her forays at the yacht club, weaved in and out among the guests, laughing, posing for pictures, and, of course, talking football. At both the party and practice, she fell into conversation with Charley Winner, the new head coach. In addition to following his father-in-law, Weeb Ewbank, in the position, Winner had also played football under Ewbank back at Washington University in St. Louis. That first year at Wash U, Ewbank issued all his halfbacks a warning: stay away from dating his daughters. The coach had a reason for the rather surprising pronouncement: when Ewbank was an assistant at Brown University, one of the halfbacks on the team had married his oldest daughter, Luanne. Winner, who also happened to be a halfback, thought to himself, "Now, why would I want to go out with any of his daughters?" The joke ended up on him—he fell in love with Ewbank's daughter Nancy and also followed his father-in-law into coaching.

But if Winner had ever needed to prove he was his own man, he'd done it already, serving his country during World War II. A radio operator and gunner, Winner was shot down during March of 1945 and taken to a German camp. There, he and the other prisoners were generally fed a meager diet of German black bread, or perhaps dehydrated soup. A delicacy was when a horse got shot, and they could have meat. For many weeks, this was Winner's reality. As a result of the ordeal, once he was released from the camp, the coach never stopped eating—and somehow managed to stay relatively trim.[iv]

But that was almost three decades in the past. The summer of '74, he had lighter concerns on his mind: the pressure of a new coaching gig, the wellbeing of the team, how to reverse the fortunes of a club that had gone 4-10 the year prior. And as he talked with Connie that summer, Winner found himself impressed. She was enthusiastic and driven, he observed, and her interest in the Jets was undeniable. Winner knew the team was opening a new facility that year at Hempstead, where they would need someone to do clerical work for the scouting department. The job was purely secretarial, but since the person would need to organize and file scouting reports, Winner felt someone with Connie's passion for football would fit well in the role.

Out of the blue, he mentioned the job to her. He explained they weren't looking for girls unfamiliar with the game who merely wanted to sit around talking on the phone.

"You really know your stuff," he acknowledged. "Would you consider working for us?"

If Winner had *written* her five-year plan essay, he couldn't have made a more perfect offer. Connie thought for less than two seconds.

"I'll be there at 5:30 in the morning if you want," she answered.

That was it—there were no second interviews, no application to agonize over. The position was hers. For $7500 a year, in her first real job out of college, she was about to become the newest secretary for her beloved New York Jets.

Woody Hayes had proved right.

CHAPTER 10

The Secretary Who Couldn't Type

When Connie arrived at the Jets complex for her first day of work—driving a special edition green-and-white Oldsmobile she'd ordered from the dealership owned by Rob Russell's father[i]—she was the only female employee in the whole building. The Jets had other secretaries at their offices in Manhattan, but at Hempstead, where the coaches, general manager, and scouting personnel were located, Connie was the lone secretary. That meant that on her first day, there was no one to give her an orientation. Someone told her where to sit—an L-shaped desk near the main entrance—and she was left to decode the rest.

That proved to be a lot. She was soon immersed in the daily struggle of juggling clerical work for the scouting department with receptionist duties for the entire complex: filing papers, answering and redirecting calls, typing documents for coaches, greeting everyone who came through the door, and putting the coffee pot on.

As far as the actual skills required for the job, she quickly realized she was, in many ways, woefully unqualified. Some parts were intuitive—there was no one more cheerful and efficient than Connie on the phone or welcoming people as they walked through the complex door. But other facets baffled her. Someone asked her to write a form letter to the commissioner of the NFL; Connie had no clue how it should be done. She scoured an encyclopedia or other reference material trying to figure out where the return address went or how many spaces to employ in the formatting. Shorthand was another obstacle. Though it was a standard method employed by secretaries when taking dictation to accurately record someone's words, Connie had never been taught the intricate vocabulary of symbols and abbreviations and found herself scrawling frantically as she tried to keep up with whoever was dictating, silently hoping she'd be able to decipher her own handwriting by the end. Pen and paper, however, were infinitely preferable to working with the typewriter, which quickly established itself as her mortal enemy. She'd used one occasionally for school papers in college, but classified ads in the '60s and '70s often sought secretaries who could type 60 words per minute—a feat so far beyond Connie's skillset that she might as well have been asked to reverse the direction of the earth spinning on its axis. Winner had just assumed she knew how to type when he offered her the job, and Connie hadn't volunteered otherwise.

Now the machine sat on her desk—an evil, unforgiving taskmaster, flaunting her mistakes in black and white. While others' fingers flew across the keys, Connie's fumbled; instead of a smooth stream of taps, they produced slow, erratic, clicks betraying her incompetence. Her best strategy, she decided, was to avoid using the machine when people were around. This was difficult, since her desk sat on the first floor right by a main door. But she armed herself with a bottle of Wite-Out and went to work. If someone came by, she usually switched to filing papers.

She wasn't the only one in the office practicing a bit of subterfuge. While the league itself had begun growing by leaps and bounds after the TV contracts of 1964, the Jets still maintained a friendly, mom-and-pop environment on the personnel side, where everyone soon became family and enthusiasm could get a person farther than previous experience.[ii] Jim Pons, who became the team's video guru, had no video background before joining the Jets. He'd been part of a music group known as the Turtles, who'd released the hit "Happy Together" and had even performed at the White House. When Pons finished his music career, he agreed to interview with the Jets as a favor to a friend and ended up accepting the job the year before Connie arrived. He worked first as a jack-of-all-trades, performing odds-and-ends duties like mailing out Joe Namath posters. Then Weeb Ewbank, finishing out his time in the team's front office, got an idea. The Jets used a film company in Manhattan to record their games on Sundays, but it took till Wednesday for the film to arrive so that the coaches could begin studying it. Down south, the Dallas Cowboys had expedited the process by building a film lab into their training center and employing their own cameraman. Ewbank wanted the same for the Jets. He'd heard Pons was from Hollywood, so he asked the former musician if he knew anything about movies. Pons had never actually done camera work, but he told Ewbank they called him Cecil B. DeMille back in Hollywood. So Ewbank gave him the gig. The championship-winning coach's instinct, while ill-informed, proved excellent—Pons thrived in the role.

One day, a petite, older lady with glasses and a halo of light, sandy-colored hair walked through the doors of the complex—how much older, Connie, who greeted her, had no idea at the time.

"Is this Eub Weebank Hall?" the visitor asked, butchering the name of the Jets legend, who was still working in the building that had been named for him.

"It's Weeb Ewbank," Connie explained, and they both laughed.

The stranger's name was Elsie Cohen, and she was there to interview for a job as the head coach's secretary. Worried she wouldn't get hired because of her age, she knocked 10 years off of it during the application process—a secret she kept guiltily from her coworkers for around a decade.

Despite their age difference, Connie and Elsie quickly became friends. Elsie wasn't into football, but she was a dear and always traipsed around the office singing, "I've got the world on a string." On Tuesdays, they stayed late together to help type up the coaches' game plans for the upcoming Sunday. During office hours, Burgess Owens, a shy but talented defensive back who had been the Jets' top draft pick the year before, often came and sat by them. Sometimes, he quietly read a book; other times, they discussed books and Hollywood, or he and Connie might deliberate about players the Jets would be facing. Connie was trustworthy, Owens felt—he could talk to her without reservation and knew she wouldn't run and tell someone else. In general, the young athlete was introverted, but Elsie and Connie always made him feel comfortable talking, and with the bubbly young secretary, the laughter flowed long.

The best part of her job, Connie soon discovered, was that she never knew who would walk through the complex doors. If the team's play on the field had sunk once more to the mediocrity of their early years, their celebrity draw had not. From athletes to actors, the complex attracted faces that lit up televisions and sports arenas for decades. Pelé—the most iconic athlete in the world, of whom it was rumored Nigeria actually paused its civil war to watch play—swung by to work out at the Jets facilities. So did New York Nets star Julius "Dr. J" Erving, sporting a sophisticated powder blue hat.[1] One day, Connie heard her childhood hero, Roy Rogers, was attending the opening of his

[1]A young girl who was playing "Annie" on Broadway also stopped by the complex in the 1970s—her name was Sarah Jessica Parker.

restaurant across the street. She hurried over, and there he was, wearing the white Stetson she'd been so sure as a little girl would appear over the horizon of her street. Now, she was able to sit down, talk with him, and even managed to get a picture of them together.

Back at the Jets complex—on a rare day—strolled one of the Jets owners, Leon Hess, through the front door, with his customary big cigar. "Hello, Connie," he'd say, and sometimes asked her help identifying players as they walked by. At the time, Hess struck her as generally hands-off on football operations, to the point where he recognized few of his own players outside of Namath. Connie, who knew the roster better than the back of her hand, was happy to oblige. She also impressed a middle-aged, charismatic Al Davis of the Oakland Raiders so much when he visited that he wanted to hire her away from the Jets. Standing there in his black leather jacket, his hair greased back, the Raiders' managing general partner spoke charmingly. "Connie," he said, "I want to make you a Raider." She would never have left her beloved Jets, but it was flattering nonetheless.

She also never knew who might call the office. One day, she picked up the phone and heard one of America's most famous voices—Howard Cosell, the Monday Night Football announcer—asking to speak with one of the coaches.

Connie explained the coach was in a meeting.

"I don't care," the broadcaster answered. "This is Howard Cosell. Don't you know who this is? Get him on the phone for me right now."

"I'm sorry, he's in a meeting," Connie tried again. "May I take a message?"

"You need to get him on the phone right now!" Cosell bellowed.

Connie stood firm.

"He's in a meeting," she insisted. "Sorry. I have to take a message."

She wasn't the only one who'd ever run afoul of Cosell's bombastic arrogance. Her father had once taken exception to remarks Cosell made about the team and Weeb Ewbank and wrote the broadcaster letters addressing the issue. One day, a very irate Cosell left a message with Dr. Cal's answering service, which the doctor used so as not to miss a patient's call. When he phoned Cosell back, the broadcaster chewed him out, insisting he was "the worst, ignorant, psychotic idiot I have come across in my professional career." Dr. Cal calmed him down, but soon the broadcaster began prodding for information. He wanted the *real* story behind a Jets player's career-damaging broken ankle, which he'd supposedly injured stepping off a curb.

"Just what is the story on how his leg was broken?" Cosell's voice had gone syrupy.

"I don't know, but if I did know, I certainly wouldn't tell you, Howard," replied Dr. Cal, his temper rising.

"You know who you are?" Cosell sneered. "You're just a poor little schnook from Long Island, who just happens to be with the New York Jets."

"Suppose I'm a rich little schnook?" Dr. Cal observed.

But later, when Connie saw Cosell at a football event, her extrovert nature got the better of her. Realizing they'd never actually met, she decided to put his past slights to her family behind her and walked up to introduce herself.

"Mr. Cosell," she began politely, "My name is Connie Nicholas. My father is Dr. Cal Nicholas, and my uncle is Dr. James Nicholas."

To which Cosell, who hadn't bothered to stand on her arrival, offered a four-word response:

"That's nice, little girl."

Connie gave up and decided he was the most obnoxious person she'd ever met.

She enjoyed it much more when fans called the Jets complex. She often engaged them in conversation, and sometimes, if she found out their favorite player, she asked them to hold the line and went dashing back toward the male-only area of the facility, calling as she pushed through a set of swinging doors:

"Girl back!"

That was her warning cry. If no one answered, she walked down the hallway and through another set of doors into the locker room.

The room itself was sparse in its makeup. The bare, cinderblock walls were painted white. A chalkboard and a clock adorned them, and an old-fashioned TV with a turn knob perched on top of a row of lockers, which didn't have doors. There was one pay phone hanging on the wall that wives or girlfriends of players might call. Down the center of the room ran an odd setup of round metal seats. In two rows, running along either side of a line of tables, the seats configured like a spine, with a seat where each vertebra would be. Guys could eat lunch there, or play cards. Pepper Burruss, a young member of the training staff, once witnessed a player dance disco on the table.

On entering, Connie walked up to the player she needed. If the fan calling was female, the player was usually dark-haired David Knight, who possessed a killer smile and wavy hair that reached almost to his shoulders.

"When you're done, can you come up front?" she asked.

He usually did, and so did the others she asked. Most players at the time even deemed it an honor to sign autographs. In those days, the athletes spent the length of their career with one or two teams, and smaller salaries meant less economic separation from their fan base, which encouraged a healthy interaction between the two. Connie also had a knack for knowing which guys to approach with a fan request, and which to let be.

A vastly different scenario was when fans believed they had a chance to *become* a player, a dream the Jets perhaps unknowingly fueled early that November—and which immediately turned Connie's work number into the hottest in town for the day.[iii]

The precipitating event had come the Sunday before, when Jets kicker Bobby Howfield was injured in a home game against Houston—another blow for a team that had won only one of eight contests that fall. Even worse, their opponent the following week was the hated New York Giants. With Howfield's status uncertain, and the upcoming Giants game the first of six left that season, the team determined they should add another kicker to its roster and made the mistake of announcing it publicly.

The Jets' phone lines ignited. Callers submerged the beleaguered secretaries at the offices in Manhattan and in Hempstead, where the main number rang Connie's desk. Everyone wanted a tryout—even an 11-year-old boy.

Connie tried to let him down gently.

"You're kind of young, aren't you?" she asked.

"Oh, it's not for me," the boy responded. "It's a surprise for my father. I don't want him to know I'm going to be the Jets kicker."

Outside her window, meanwhile, two college-age boys were kicking a football around. But the girl who came out of the building, and to whom they appealed, hoping for a tryout, was no football greenhorn. If they'd been nailing 40 yarders, Connie might've said something to Charley Winner or Jets assistant general manager Mike Martin, but she'd noticed they'd only managed to kick the ball a pathetic 10 to 15 yards at best. She merely told them, however—along with a third boy who'd joined them—that she thought the Jets already had a kicker.

By the end of the day, she'd fielded fifty-three calls from people wanting a tryout. She passed the handful of legitimate ones on to the assistant general manager. Her old friend Paul Zimmerman, meanwhile, did a story on the caller fiasco for the *New York Post* and interviewed her for it. "Connie," he wrote in the piece, "is 'hip' on football." The team ultimately went with a free agent named Pat Leahy, who stayed with the franchise for 18 years. He even brought the luck of the

Irish with him that first season, because the Jets beat the Giants 26–20 in overtime the following week and didn't lose another game the rest of the year.

Altogether, it was exhilarating being at the complex, talking football all day—with Ewbank (now the general manager), the trainers, the equipment manager, even the fans who called. She gleaned a lot from Mike Holovak (now coaching the offensive backs), who'd been an All-American in high school and college and had himself played in the NFL for a time. When Holovak looked at a player, he ultimately boiled his assessment down to one all-encompassing question: *can he play football?* Some evaluators got caught up in statistics, dazzled by a player's height, weight, and speed. Holovak considered numbers, but he refused to be enslaved by them. Instead, he probed deeper: *Is he productive? Does he make plays? What's his heart like?* Connie soaked up the information, and Holovak indulged her questions. Like others before him, he never made her feel any less because she was a woman asking questions.

All the while, she did her best to manage her volume of work. Her receptionist and various secretarial demands made it difficult to keep up with the scouting department paperwork. Player evaluations poured into the Jets' office at Hempstead, only to stack up on her desk until she could read through and organize them for later reference by team personnel. Her office hours stretched to seven or eight each evening. The next NFL draft would take place at the end of January, one month after the regular season ended. She couldn't afford to get behind.

CHAPTER 11

The First Female Scout

They were all waiting on her.

The men in the room were waiting. In New York City, the NFL was waiting. Beyond that, twenty-six teams across the country were waiting—waiting for her decision, but she couldn't think about that.

She had to think fast.

She'd left for the office that morning before the sun came up—the second day of the 1975 draft, a grueling 17-round marathon in late January. Holovak, who'd soon take over the scouting department as director of player personnel, was part of the group that assembled in a large room at the complex that morning. Connie's role was strictly clerical: whenever the Jets made a selection, she reached for the landline phone perched atop a small table where she was stationed and placed the call to the team's representatives at the draft headquarters in New York City so they could pass the information on to the league: "The New York Jets select ..."

The New York Jets select Anthony Davis, University of Southern California.

The New York Jets select Richard Wood, University of Southern California.

On and on they'd gone, for 16 rounds already. To others, it may have been grueling, but Connie thought it was the best two days of the year.

They had reached the final round, a place where finding talent amounted to a roll of the dice. Even in earlier rounds, the draft was virtually an elaborate guessing game—one looked at the information available and tried to predict how a young man might be in a year, or five, or ten from now, while playing a game at a level he'd never played before. "The draft is like Christmas," Charley Winner once said. "You get all these good-looking packages, and then you wait and have to open them up at training camp, and that's when you really find out what they can do." It was the business of predicting people, which was risky. One could measure height and weight and 40-yard dashes. One couldn't measure heart.

As personnel in the room prepared to make their last decision that day on the future of their franchise, an idea came to Holovak. Or maybe he'd had it for a while, mulling it over in his thoughts. When it came time for the final selection, he looked at Connie.

In fact, all of the coaches in the room were looking at her.

"Connie," Holovak said, "You get to make the last pick."

No one in the room objected.

With the team still on the clock, she thought swiftly.

The Jets, she knew, needed wide receivers. Her mind traveled to the Ohio State roster—Mike Bartoszek, a wide receiver/tight end, had been on the team during her last two years at Ohio State and played in three consecutive Rose Bowls. "Good athletic ability," his scouting reports had read. Though his numbers weren't impressive, she knew he was well coached and from a quality program.

Connie recommended he be given a chance. The personnel in the room ultimately agreed.

For the final time that day, she picked up the phone and called the NFL in New York to submit the pick—only this time, it was her own.

"The New York Jets," she said, "select Mike Bartoszek."

Bartoszek's selection was the first time, to anyone's knowledge, a woman had made a draft pick in the NFL and called it in. When he arrived on the Jets' campus later that year, tanned and trim with a mop of golden-brown hair, she got a picture of him at the complex as he stood in the hallway wearing an Ohio State shirt. He failed to make the team's final roster, but so did 15 of the other 16 players the Jets drafted that year (in fact, Bartoszek fared better than some, since he was not the first player cut at camp). Only linebacker Richard Wood and center Joe Fields, taken in the third and 14th rounds, respectively, made the team.[i]

After that momentous occasion on draft day, however, nothing changed for Connie—at first. She returned to filing papers and greeting the myriad of people who came through the complex. Sometimes, Joe Namath stopped by her desk to autograph the posters fans sent him. He personalized everything; even when fans handed him something to sign, he always asked their name. Connie, meanwhile, was proud as punch to do anything for him. One of her favorite habits was baking an apple pie (using Lynne's recipe) and bringing it into the office for him. Being able to reserve the whole pie for himself, however, was beyond his capabilities; even the great Joe Namath couldn't guarantee a pie's safety if carried past the cadre of hungry football players in the locker room.

In early 1975, not long after Connie selected Bartoszek in the draft, a new general manager arrived from Dallas. Al Ward, who'd been with the Cowboys for almost 10 years, was a handsome man with graying hair and a slight, charming drawl who fell in quickly with the Jets office family. He had a handball court put into the complex, and he and coaches often played as a way to stay in shape.

Connie also had her first major gaffe at the office. One afternoon, when traveling secretary John Free had dropped off her and Elsie's paychecks at their desks, Connie opened hers and saw she'd received a raise. It was her first as a young professional.

"Elsie!" she cried, her excitement bubbling over. "What did you get? I got a raise!"

Elsie answered quietly.

"I didn't get one."

Instantly, Connie realized her mistake. Horrified and guilt-ridden, she confessed her blunder to Mr. Free, who'd known the Nicholas family for ages and still treated her like a little girl.

When she finished, his assessment was harsh.

"You did that?" he demanded.

"Yes," she admitted.

"That's very awful," he scolded. "That's a horrible thing that you did. Now you go into Mr. Ward, and you tell him what a terrible thing you did."

Tell the general manager? The idea was petrifying. No piano-recital stage fright could have prepared her for this ignominy. With trepidation, Connie approached Ward's office. The new general manager listened while she repeated her confession.

But this time, no harsh words awaited her when she finished.

"Connie," he reassured his young employee, "That's OK. We all make mistakes. These things happen. Don't worry about it."

Relief swept over her, as she realized everything would be all right. Even better, Elsie, with true class, never held the incident against her. They remained close and sometimes joined a few others for dinner at Heads & Tails, the steak and seafood restaurant owned by Elsie's son. Since moving home, Connie had discovered—for the first time in her adult life—that she could eat three meals a day and maintain her weight. The way she presented herself was also finding its stride; she'd long since shed her disinterest in clothes and preferred tasteful, figure-flattering garments—in green and white, if at all possible. Later, a coach she once worked with at the club happened to mention to his wife how well he thought Connie dressed. "She immediately ran up a $254 clothing bill," he wrote to Connie. "You can rest assured my compliments will go directly to you in the future."

Added to all this eventually was a second procedure on her nose; a cartilage bump had grown on it, so this time, Connie went to a plastic surgeon and had both the bump removed and the feature tweaked. Afterwards, for the first time in her life, she was happy with her nose and felt beautiful.

But if her outward appearance had found its stride, there was learning elsewhere. At the time, drinking and driving was a common practice, and while Connie wasn't a heavy drinker, she made a poor choice one evening after socializing with other Jets staffers at Heads & Tails. They'd had a marvelous time, and just as she stood to leave, Joe Namath walked in and saw her.

"Come on," he said congenially, as a way of inviting her to join him.

No person—sober or otherwise—would turn down a chance to socialize with Namath, so Connie sat down again, this time at Namath's booth, and they started talking. Others soon joined them. Connie consumed another Harvey Wallbanger—her go-to drink, since she wasn't a fan of wine and avoided beer because Lynne always insisted smoking or drinking beer looked "unfeminine"—and subsequently rendered herself unfit to get behind the wheel. She did, anyway, and somehow made the half-hour drive home without incident. But when she arrived, her parents could tell she'd gone past her limit. They yelled at her all the way up the stairs—a sobering memory for the young professional, who learned from her mistake.

With more personnel being added at the Jets' Hempstead location, she was soon able to move into the large, open room where Mike Holovak worked. Holovak had become her immediate boss after taking over as director of player personnel that year. They shared the space with a few other employees, including another young woman, Gail Baldwin, who'd been hired to provide administrative support to the general manager. Since the role required dealing with player contracts, the Jets had wanted someone with a legal background in the job; Gail, who'd returned to the area to take care of her father after he suffered a serious accident, had worked for an attorney before joining the team. The Jets had to build a counter around her desk—located in an area behind the door—to help prevent anyone swinging by (including the press) from catching a glimpse of the contracts. The team had also added a gentleman named Pete Marasco to the player personnel department—he'd pioneered some of the earliest draft ratings and collected information on players all across the country. Connie and Pete got along well; they were two of a kind in their obsession with the draft and knowledge of players.

The new arrangement put Connie in the thick of the scouting department. Scouts spent most of their time on the road, but what remained of the department at the complex was centered in that room, and when the scouts returned, they gathered there.

Now, in addition to the reports she helped organize and file, Connie was immersed in the conversations about the players. One time, the general manager was chatting with a scout in the room when someone, talking on the phone, yelled across to another scout about a certain linebacker:

"What's his time in the 40?"

But it was Connie's voice that came back in response.

"4.7."

Ward was stunned. After that, he began paying more attention to her.

To certain people within the organization, her passion for evaluating personnel was well known. Frank Ramos, who worked in the team's public relations department, heard from coworkers about her work ethic and deep interest in player evaluations—she asked questions of scouts and coaches, building her knowledge on how one assessed players or became a scout. She and Mike Holovak had long talks about football—even when they disagreed, Holovak treated her opinion with respect. The young woman even "talked scout," Ward later noted, using inside terminology she'd picked up from other scouts, who might toss out slang like "COD" for "change of direction" when discussing a defensive back. Those who attended personnel meetings where Connie took notes admitted to Ward they went to Connie to ask about a player's stats, like his time in the 40-yard dash—in most cases, she had the answer without looking it up. When Ward spoke to other scouts about her, the message was always the same: they loved and respected her.

This alone was revolutionary. In that era, a woman in a football office usually meant one of two things: she pushed papers, or she owned part of the franchise (one of the Jets owners, in fact, was a lady named Helen Dillon). For a woman to be taken seriously in football matters was a challenge. And not every woman wanted to be; Elsie was content to leave football behind when she left the office for the day. "Bastions of testosterone," one trainer described the environment of a football organization at the time. Not only were the scouting departments men's clubs, but they were also by nature closed-off, exclusive entities, for teams guarded their scouting secrets jealously.

Yet here was Connie, fitting in, in a world where she was never supposed to be. Holovak by now was in his mid-to-late fifties, and, Ward knew, not overly easy to convince. And yet, when the two men talked about Connie, the former All-American told Ward, "If somebody ever breaks the [gender] line in scouting, it's probably going to be Connie."

Ward could have left it at that. He opted not to.

After about a year, bolstered by the groundswell of support within the department, he made a gutsy, historic offer. Sitting at a long table with Holovak and several others, eating dinner, Ward and Connie began talking of what she wanted to do in her career.

"Connie," he said, "Would you like to be a scout for the Jets?"

There was, of course, only one answer she would ever give.

"Yes," she answered, stunned.

"You're in," Ward answered.

The moment was extraordinary, but, in keeping with the times, devoid of fanfare. The Jets didn't make a huge public fuss over the decision, although Dick Young, the legendary writer for the *Daily News* and the *Sporting News*, later included a brief mention of the development in one of his columns: "Connie Nicholas is the first woman scout for an NFL team," he wrote. "She has been eyeing Big 10 talent for the Jets. Her dad, Dr. Calvin Nicholas, is the Jets' internist. Her uncle is the famed Jim Nicholas, orthopedic pioneer in sports surgery. Connie's front-office associates call her 'The Girl Scout.'"[ii]

Much like when she was hired, Connie slid into her new situation competently and quietly. She kept her primary duties as the department secretary—indeed, that remained her main job—but added to that now was the ability to evaluate and grade player films and travel to various schools for in-person evaluations, as her secretarial duties permitted.

Not long after the change, Ward attended an owners' meeting and mentioned that he'd given Connie Nicholas some scouting responsibilities. The owners—who'd known the Nicholas family for years—accepted the bold move with minimal questioning.

At only twenty-four years old, less than three years out of school, Connie Nicholas had become the first female scout in the fifty-five year history of the NFL.

That spring, she made a scouting trip back to Ohio State.

For most scouts, the bulk of their time was spent on the flight paths and roadways that connected them to America's football talent. A scout could always plan on two things at work: travel and being wrong at least once about a player. In general, the job required threading a delicate line between conviction and hubris—a scout needed enough confidence in his opinion to go to bat for a player, while also being aware that the final call on whom the team drafted would likely never be his to make. Overall, the job demanded plenty of work for little public recognition—work that required tight lips. When one pro scout started in the business during the late '70s, he asked for some advice. "Keep your mileage, and keep your mouth shut," was the response.

In the 1970s, scouting was a clunky technological process. When Jets scouts traveled, they often lugged blank evaluation forms along with their projectors, used to watch film a college had of its players. Once at a school, a scout would try to observe a player at practice and analyze whatever 16-millimeter film of him the institution had available. Sometimes, schools only had one copy of the film, since it was expensive to develop and duplicate. Plus, by mid-October, nearly everyone had watched the same film and it often broke, needing to be repaired. The film might contain a player's best game, or his worst—a frustrating roulette for the evaluator, who often got only one shot to observe a player. For the athlete himself, overall exposure throughout the season was fairly limited, as only a few college games made it onto the TV schedule each week.

But dissecting video was just one part of the job. Scouts were also detectives—they had to ferret out information about a player not easily accessible to those living outside his vicinity or hometown. Trainers, Connie knew, were one of the most important assets on any team, college or pro, and a valuable resource for the type of information scouts sought. They were with the players every day and witnessed them at their toughest and most vulnerable states. Scouts who had "ins" or connections at a school could talk to them and discover gems: "This guy tends to be a complainer," they might warn; "This guy's hurt a lot," or, "This guy gives you everything he's got, no matter how badly he's hurt." Knowing the coach at a premiere, closed-off program like Ohio State, as Connie did, was considered a great "in"— Hayes would talk to her about anyone and anything, as well as let her talk to just about anyone in his program.

On this trip, her scouting work for the Jets created a miniature splash—the campus newspaper published a feature on her. "Ohio State woman grad now part-time Jets scout," read the headline. "Today she is secretary to Mike Holovak in the Jets' player personnel department," the piece noted, "and though nothing is definite yet, she could very well be moving into scouting full time in the near future. Were that to happen, she would be a majority of one." The article ran beside a picture of her, taken as she sat, her head turned slightly like an old-fashioned painting, her slender frame clad in a businesslike dress with green and white stripes.

On returning to New York, she received a letter from Ohio State's associate dean and director of the home economics program:

> *Dear Connie:*
>
> *If I were to cite the home economics education graduate with the most unusual occupation, you might be the winner! The story in the Lantern seemed well done—I hope you were pleased. Best regards to you, and the next time you visit Columbus I hope you will stop by to see Dr. Bailey and me.*
>
> *Sincerely,*
>
> *Francille M. Firebaugh*

Connie knew, however, that trips to Columbus were not going to be frequent for the time being. Whereas other scouts spent the bulk of their time traveling, she still had her main administrative duties back at the office (when *she* filed scouting reports, she was essentially handing them to herself to file). But working at the complex also brought a unique advantage to her scouting. She established the habit of walking outside to observe the team practice, much as she'd done at Ohio State, so that she could keep learning. As a result, she was intimately familiar with the team's playbook, a luxury most scouts' travel schedule made impossible. The playbook, after all, was the coaches' department; their focus was personnel. But Connie, who spent her time watching the Jets rather than an ever-changing lineup of college teams each week, witnessed all of the moving parts come together and could assess the overall picture. The rest of the scouts often only had that chance when they stopped by training camp in the summer.

That April of 1976, the Jets drafted a Penn State linebacker named Greg Buttle in the third round, but playing in the college All-Star game forced him to miss the start of camp that summer. Anxious someone would beat him out of a roster spot, he kept calling Connie—whom he'd met while visiting the team after the draft—to check up on the competition.

"How do you think the other linebackers look?" he'd ask. "What do you think my chances are?"

"Don't worry," she reassured him each time. "In my opinion, you're not going to have a problem."

Her advice was solid—not only did Buttle make the roster that year, but he even started that preseason against the despised Giants and played every game his rookie season.

Lean years, sadly, had come to the franchise's on-field performance. The team had not returned to the playoffs since the year following their Super Bowl triumph; as the '70s progressed, their play sank into a quagmire worse than their Titans days. One ray of hope had come in the second half of the '74 season, when they strung together six consecutive wins, but their poor start ultimately doomed them to another year without the playoffs. Namath was growing old, though that didn't stop the newly formed World Football League from trying to woo him the following year with a $4 million paycheck. Phillip Iselin, one of the Jets owners, handed out business cards with the phrase, "I'll be damned if I know," when people asked what Namath would do or what was wrong with the franchise.[iii] Namath ultimately stayed, but so did the losses.

Monday mornings were difficult, dreary times for those in the office around the coaching staff. Connie, though she kept up a perky front, felt the same intense misery after a loss as she had when a little girl; now, too, was the added worry for the coaches' jobs, which they might be in danger of losing, and the ripple effect on their wives and children. The fans could sulk for a whole week following a defeat, but the players, for their sanity, frequently had to take a different approach. Dr. Cal, as he examined them on Tuesday mornings, was always amazed by how they'd already seemed to discard the baggage of the previous Sunday. They had to. It was their job. They couldn't prepare for their next opponent if their emotions remained invested in the past.

But change was inevitable. Near the end of the '75 season, the Jets released Charley Winner as head coach. In the office, Connie and Elsie sobbed—it was like losing family. Winner handed over a ball he used while playing at the handball court to Buddy Ryan—Gerry Philbin's old coach at the University of Buffalo, who now worked for the Jets.

"You'll need this," Winner told him.

"Charley," Ryan answered, "I won't have anyone to beat anymore."[iv]

Needing a shot of optimism, the Jets turned to the college ranks and found one of the most cheery, optimistic men in the sport's history: a short, blond-haired gentleman with big-rimmed glasses who'd been coaching at North Carolina State. He was an excellent collegiate coach, but a determined Leon Hess coaxed and ultimately convinced him to try the pros. The man's name was Lou Holtz.

The new coach soon set about changing the team's identity. He released or traded several veterans and emphasized building through the draft over exchanging picks for other teams' veteran talent, something Charley Winner had not been opposed to. "I don't think bringing in older players is the answer," Holtz told a reporter. "If they're that good, then why are the other clubs looking to get rid of them?"[v]

Holtz was personable; he answered every letter he received (even from people he didn't know) and often dictated his responses to Elsie, who jotted them down in shorthand before typing them up. He appeared almost professorial around the complex, with his cup of tea and his pipe. But he also knew how to inspire people—his record at the collegiate level had been impeccable for helping distressed programs become winners. A young coach by the name of Joe Gardi, who'd lost his coaching position when the World Football League folded, was so determined to get a job that he kept calling the complex when Holtz was assembling his coaching staff. Connie took a message from Gardi and passed it on to Holtz. But Gardi kept calling, calling,

calling. Finally, Connie couldn't take it anymore and hung up on him. When Holtz eventually did hire Gardi, Connie and the new special teams coach had a good laugh later at their inauspicious beginning.

It was the season, however, for unpromising starts. The Jets played their first four games on the road that year and returned home winless. Tragedy also struck the team during their game in Denver. Dr. Cal, on rare road trip with the club since Dr. Jim was indisposed, was in the locker room at halftime when Helen Dillon came in and said fellow owner Phil Iselin, also in Denver for the game, had taken suddenly and seriously ill. Dr. Cal dashed all the way to the farthest part of the stadium—the upper deck near the end zone—where Iselin had been situated in an enclosed box. The owner had just been taken to the hospital by the emergency team.

Dr. Cal met up with the Jets contingent at the hospital. Mrs. Dillon's husband, who was also a doctor, described the cardiac arrest that had seized the owner. Dr. Dillon had ultimately sustained Iselin for fifteen to twenty minutes before the emergency team arrived. While the hospital treated Iselin, and the owner's wife stoically waited, Dr. Cal kept Leon Hess, back in New York, informed. By morning, Iselin had stabilized. He eventually returned to New York and in late November had recovered well enough to attend the team's annual Thanksgiving dinner at Shea.

By then, the Jets' season was a disaster. Holtz had worked valiantly to implement a collegiate-like approach on and off the field, but the plan was fraught with difficulty. In college, a coach could recruit the kind of players that responded to his coaching; in the pros, one had to work with the players already there, who, instead of being impressionable, 18- to 22-year-old students bursting with school pride, were men in their twenties and thirties coming to work each morning. Holtz, hoping to recreate the vibrant passion of a collegiate atmosphere, even penned a Jets fight song; the attempt fell flat. He tried having quarterback Richard Todd, Namath's heir apparent, run a wishbone-style offense, which had been vastly successful during Holtz's tenure at North Carolina State. That, too, tanked.

The failures weighed on the new coach.[vi] Unhappiness was etched on his face and seemed reflected in the weather as the dreary New York winter arrived. A long, lonely and chilly off-season was coming—the players gone, the building turned over to the administration. And yet, in early December, before the season ended, Holtz told the Jets he would finish out his five-year contract.

But the next day, he walked out of his office and called to Connie. There had been a glow about him when he'd arrived at work that day.

"I'm gonna resign," he revealed.

Connie was stunned. Heartbroken, she managed to say something about wishing he wouldn't leave. She didn't ask why he was doing so, because she didn't feel it was her place. She recognized the decision must have been difficult, for she knew Holtz liked finishing what he started. But he was happy again, and she was happy for him. She gave him a daughterly hug.

Holtz departed the Jets with a 3–10 record, and Mike Holovak coached the final game of the year, where the team got creamed 42–3 by the Bengals at Shea. Connie watched, as she always did, a nervous wreck. Growing up, she'd only been able to stomach a piping hot knish at the stadium on the mornings before games; even now, as an adult, she could barely eat before kickoff. She sometimes took her friend Eileen Matthews, another huge sports fan, with her to the stadium, and the two spent the afternoon cheering loudly for the team. Afterwards, they met her parents along with several, if not all, of the guests whom Dr. Cal invited to the game for dinner at the Diamond Club, where he insisted on paying for everyone's meal. Finally, there, Connie was able to eat.

Despite the devastating loss of Holtz, and her heartfelt emotion over the Jets' season, things were going well for her professionally. In the scouting department, her opinion continued eliciting respect as the team prepared for the upcoming draft. At one point, they were arguing the merits of a projected late-round pick named Dan Alexander out of Louisiana State University. Holovak liked him, but other guys weren't convinced.

So Holovak took a different tack.

"Well, ask Connie," he offered. "She likes him."

No one laughed at the remark. Alexander soon inched up the Jets' draft list, and when the draft arrived, the Jets selected him in the eighth round. He turned out to be a steal, playing for the franchise for thirteen seasons.

She also went on a scouting trip that New Year's to the Orange Bowl, held in the same stadium where, as an ebullient high school senior, she'd watched the Jets win their first—and only—Super Bowl. This time, from the stands, she evaluated a defensive lineman for the University of Colorado as he battled Hayes's Ohio State squad. There were two main components to the scouting report: ranking the player's technique via a numerical grading scale—(1) Excellent, (2) Good, (3) Above Average, (4) Average, and (5) Poor—and a comment section where she could expound on a player's strengths and weaknesses and record information shared by coaches and trainers. In the eight relevant technique categories, Connie graded him "above average" or higher: quickness off the ball, strength, lateral movement, tackle, pursuit, balance, pass rush, and one-on-one capabilities.

Below, in the comment area, she described what she saw:

> *Was impressed with him in Orange Bowl till he got hurt—clogged up middle well for them—takes on blocker & pursues well—strong & tough tackler—not a top three or four rounds but solid middle choice—when he got hurt, OSU ran up the middle a lot more & with more success.*

Sitting there in the stands, pen and scouting report in hand, it was as if she'd come full circle—her beloved Woody Hayes on the sideline below, the flash of helmets before her, the pleasant ghosts of Super Bowl memories hanging in the air. A little girl's infatuation had matured into a young woman's vibrant, energetic passion, one that had opened doors beyond her wildest hopes and resulted in accomplishing what no other woman had done before.

But she was about to discover something—or someone—even greater.

CHAPTER 12

Romance

The first time Connie saw him was at the hotel restaurant.

It wasn't her regular lunch spot. She often went to the diner not far from the Jets complex and ordered a healthy mix of greens and feta cheese, which the employees there had taken to calling the "Connie salad." But today, she broke with routine and went to the Holiday Inn-Westbury, where she ordered a Reuben sandwich.

The restaurant was crowded that afternoon; in fact, all the tables were filled. A tall, good-looking man with brown hair and a moustache came in and made his way to the cash register. Connie, walking by in her green sweater dress with heeled boots, caught his attention. He thought her figure was stunning.

"How are you?" he ventured in passing.

He looked a little like her childhood crush, Bake Turner.

"Good, how are you?" Connie answered.

But that was virtually the end of their exchange. His food paid for, he left the restaurant.

Connie finished her lunch and walked out to the lobby, where a basketball team staying at the hotel had gathered. Feeling chatty, she struck up a conversation. She kept an eye out for the handsome stranger she'd noticed at lunch, but he never reappeared. And she wanted him to.

Not ready to give up, she decided to saunter down to the lower level, ostensibly to use the ladies' room (even though there was one on the floor where she'd been talking). She didn't see the mystery man as she came down the steps, nor had he appeared by the time she re-emerged.

Realizing she should head back to work, Connie started back up the stairs.

Suddenly, she saw him—sprinting down the hallway toward her. He'd been in one of the rooms, preparing for a seminar he was teaching that afternoon, and by chance had stepped outside and noticed her on the stairway. When he finally reached her, he spoke.

"Are you taking a course here?" he asked.

"No," she answered. "I'm Connie–I'm with the Jets."

There was one question foremost in her mind, so she plunged boldly.

"Are you married?" she asked.

"No."

"All the good ones are," she explained.

Since he wasn't, they exchanged numbers. His name was John Carberg. He lived about 55 minutes away and had just recently taken a job with World-Wide

Volkswagen Porsche Audi. Connie returned to the office, feeling there was something special about him.

They set up a first date, but John got nervous and broke it. They got together not long after that, however, and hit it off immediately. John loved her attitude—she never seemed to have a bad day. Connie, meanwhile, knew from the moment their lips touched on that first date: he was the one.

Armed with this knowledge, she invited him over for dinner—an ambitious move, since despite her baking skills and home economics major, she was clueless on how to cook an entrée—or virtually anything else. Her mother came to her rescue. Before she and Dr. Cal vacated the premises, Lynne had steak seasoned in a pan, the salad chopped, and corn on the cob already in a pot on the stove for her daughter. Despite Connie's trepidation, the dinner proved a success. John soon realized there was something different about this girl; the company frequently put him up in hotels for work, where it was easy to meet women, yet he readily made the two-hour round trip to the Nicholas house and back—he *wanted* to work toward a relationship with her.

Still, he was nervous. Twelve years older than she, he was also a recovering alcoholic, twice divorced, had a young daughter, and was embroiled in the whirlwind of starting a new job. His whole life had just changed drastically. He hadn't expected to fall in love, too. Later on, he'd jokingly disparage himself to Connie with the line, "What a gem the daughter of the doctor of the New York Jets is getting." Connie, however, could never view him solely through the filter of his past struggles. She saw the depth of his goodness, too—a man rich in heart and personality.

But when it came time to buy her a birthday gift that May and eventually help her move from her parents' house into a place with her friend Eileen, John felt he was getting in too deep. By June, they'd broken up.

Still, he couldn't resist calling. He called a miserable Connie seven times over a three-week period. On one of those calls, he said, "I love you," for the first time. Connie, madly in love herself, kept the door open a little. By August, they were back together.

She'd discovered early that he rooted for the New York Giants; this was, of course, unacceptable, so she'd begun working to convert him to permanent Jets fandom. One weekend, when the team was on the road, he drove an hour to the Nicholas house to surprise her and watch the game with her and her family. He parked his car—since he worked for Porsche Audi, he always drove nice cars, though any favorable impression was lost on Connie, since she knew nothing about them—and walked to the door.

But when Connie answered his knock and saw him standing there, her face visibly fell. She *never* watched a Jets game on TV with "civilians." She couldn't help thrilling that he'd driven an hour as a surprise to be with her, but she was terribly worried he'd say something stupid about the game.

John, for his part, felt fairly comfortable that he wouldn't. And he proved right—they watched the game together, and, to Connie's amazement, he didn't say one stupid thing about it. He also got along splendidly with her grandmother, Mimi, who was visiting that afternoon (they'd bonded earlier that year over the correct way to eat lobster), although Mimi kept leaving the room and hesitating to return, afraid she was jinxing the team. Connie, for her part, had always been a little at odds with Mimi. It was peculiar, for there was plenty to like: she was the kind of grandmother who called every little kid pumpkin and attended all her grandchildren's sports games. Tragedy had struck Mimi early in life—she'd lost her parents at a young age, and a sister had drowned; Mimi had helped raise her two remaining siblings before marrying Dziadzie. In the early years, they had been dirt poor before making a small fortune in a fire extinguisher business. But past trials had failed to make Mimi bitter; she adored children and cooked every grandchild's favorite meal when they visited. Yet it had been Dziadzie, Connie felt, who truly understood her. As a kid, whenever she hit a sour note practicing the piano while Mimi babysat, the inevitable refrain was grandmother's voice calling out a correction from somewhere in the house, "A-*flat*!" (Mimi herself could play anything on the piano by ear.) She remembered being exasperated when Mimi used to swing by the house with a handful of new dresses or skirts she'd made for her granddaughter, because it meant Connie had to stop whatever sports game she was playing to go in and have them hemmed. "Just for a minute, let me put it on real quick," Mimi would beg, as she got down on her hands and knees and pinned the hem to her granddaughter's specifications. Connie stood, stewing with an ungratefulness that later made her burn with shame, dying to get back outside. But now, for the first time in her life, thanks to John, Connie began to truly appreciate Mimi.

She got along with his family, too. John, who loved practical jokes (he once prank-called Mimi, where he intoned, in a low voice, "This is the kissing bandit"), told his parents at first that his new girlfriend was the daughter of potato farmers, since, years ago, Long Island had been known for growing potatoes. It was Connie who had to tell them the story was a myth. She and John would sometimes visit the Carbergs at their big Victorian home in Connecticut, where Connie discovered another hurdle. The food consumed by the family had one ingredient in common: sugar. Even the strawberries were bathed in it. Connie, trying to eat healthily, decided to bring her own heads of lettuce. Gathered around the table for the first time with the whole family, she reached for the Italian dressing and gave the bottle a vigorous shake. Oily liquid sprayed all over the table. Connie was mortified, but the Carbergs showed themselves true family—they loved her anyway.

Even more important, she made friends with John's young daughter. Ten-year-old Lisa hadn't known what to think at first of her father having a girlfriend. But Connie proved so kind and beautiful and slender and well-dressed that Lisa was smitten. But she was also encouraging—she helped Lisa feel like she could accomplish anything she set her mind to. Connie herself had the most glamorous job in the world, Lisa thought. Whenever the young professional visited, she brought Jets memorabilia with her and distributed it among the family, although she took a good ribbing from the few Patriots fans embedded therein.

It took time, meanwhile, before Connie invited John to a Jets game, but when she did, they fell into the habit of going early and eating breakfast at the stadium's Diamond Club restaurant, although they were so in love during that first year of dating that they never finished a meal when they went out to eat. Other times, they drove up to Stonington Village, Connecticut, for a weekend getaway—a beautiful place lined by cobblestone streets. John, who had an excellent voice, sang Frank Sinatra tunes on the way up in the car. Connie liked playing Barry Manilow's "Weekend in New England."

For the first time in her life, she felt *she* was enough. John certainly admired her physical attributes, but he also made her feel she was worth more than that. In fact, he had no idea why Connie wasn't more confident in herself. She was so personable that everyone she met fell in love with her right away; it was almost a phenomenon. He'd never seen anything like it. Both were truly, passionately in love.

But by October, he felt they needed to slow down and told her so. The breakup call came at 12:15 am the next day. To make their separation actually stick this time, he began assuming a churlish demeanor, as if he couldn't stand her. Connie had no idea he'd realized it was the only way he could keep himself from rushing back. Yet this self-imposed hiatus threatened to be as fruitless as the first one--neither could resist calling the other occasionally to check in.

In the meantime, Elsie consoled her young coworker.

"Stuck is stuck," she told Connie. "He calls more often than people that are going together. Don't worry. Stuck is stuck."

Even John's mother was reassuring—she told Connie that she had nothing to worry about. But Connie was distraught and kept brainstorming ways to stay connected with John. Familiar with his morning commute and his listening habits, she called Ellie Dylan, a DJ at a local radio station.

"I know he's driving between these hours," Connie explained, and asked if Ellie could play all of her and John's songs.

Ellie readily agreed.

"Nobody else is calling at 5:30 to 8 o'clock in the morning, asking for requests," she said. "I'll be glad to."

That Thursday, John, driving into New York for work, heard one of his and Connie's songs come on the radio. Another followed. Then a third.

One after the other, as if creating their own unchained melody, all their songs played.

God is telling me that this is the girl, John thought, stunned.

Even this unmistakable sign, however, was not enough to reunite the couple by Thanksgiving; they spent the holiday apart, although Connie called John that evening. He called twice that Saturday, and she called back once. The next morning, she felt so down about their status that she did the unthinkable—she stayed home from the Jets game.

But the decision proved providential. John called.

"Let's get together," he suggested, but with a caveat: "We're just going to be friends."

Connie thought it sounded wonderful. While the Jets battled the Steelers in a tight-scoring affair at Shea Stadium, she and John went to eat at a restaurant near her house. By the time the tete-a-tete finished, they were back together.

But football, of course, was never far away from Connie's life. The house she shared with Eileen was located in Point Lookout, the easternmost tip of a southern Long Island peninsula nestled between the ocean and bay. They'd taken over the place from a Jets player who'd been cut from the team and was looking for someone to fill his lease (Point Lookout was a beach town, which made it easy for the players to rent homes there during the football season, since the properties weren't as busy as they were in the summer months.) John, visiting frequently, saw how Connie's football work was a constant labor of love. She even set up a projector at home, and their "date nights" consisted of studying game film, with an intense Connie running the film backward and forward, backward and forward again, jotting down notes on the players as she watched. During the lead-up to the draft, Eileen came home and found her poring over thick, loose-leaf binders brimming with information on college players to help her prepare.

She'd also kept in touch with Lou Holtz, who was now the head football coach at the University of Arkansas. Not long before, he'd returned to the area for a speaking engagement, and Connie, who'd never had a chance to attend one of his famous motivational speeches, decided she had to hear him. She was still living at home then and drove an hour and a half from the Nicholas house on Long Island to the event in New Jersey. The speech was absolutely fantastic, but by the time everyone had finished asking questions and she prepared to leave, it was around 11 o'clock, and. darkness had settled outside.

Holtz was worried for her.

"Connie," he insisted, "you can't drive this late at night by yourself, an hour and a half back home."

So Holtz got in his car and followed her the entire drive back to the Nicholas house. When they arrived, Dr. Cal and Lynne were still up, so Holtz visited with them over a cup of tea. Bruce, returning from a date, walked into the kitchen, saw the coach, and nearly fell over. Holtz eventually got back in his car for the hour and a half commute to his hotel, which he reached around 3:30 am. But it was quite worth the drive, he kindly assured Connie via letter after returning to Arkansas, to visit with her family.

She'd also received a call from another old acquaintance not long after she'd begun scouting—her high school basketball teacher, Mrs. Sohl. Mrs. Sohl was taking a graduate-level class for administration and physical education and asked if Connie would speak to her fellow students for a project she was doing on sports publicity. Connie readily agreed.

On the appointed day, she arrived at the classroom in Brentwood, Long Island. Mrs. Sohl, one of only a handful of women enrolled in the class of around 100 students, noticed the skeptical looks among her peers as she introduced this bubbly young woman with brown eyes and great legs.

"I'd like to introduce to you the woman who was the first female scout," Mrs. Sohl began.

The predominantly male audience exchanged glances. Was this a joke? Several of them coached football; the idea that a woman could be a scout was as implausible as one knowing as much as they did about the sport.

Mrs. Sohl continued.

"I think you're going to be very surprised when you see and hear about all that she knows and what she can do and what she has seen," she offered.

Connie got up and began her presentation. Along with unmistakable passion whenever she talked football, she also had an easy, unassuming delivery that sprang from confidence in her knowledge of the subject. When she moved on to the question and answer period, hands went up, and a barrage of questions awaited—on anything and everything football-related. Connie parried back, unflustered. Whatever the students asked, she had an answer. Now Mrs. Sohl saw her classmates turn to each other in admiration.

That's my girl up there, her former coach beamed.

When Connie finished, the applause was thunderous. A few of the men in the class even approached Mrs. Sohl.

"We're really surprised," they admitted. "We thought in the beginning, *how could a woman be a scout?* Who'd ever heard of such a thing?

"Well," they concluded, "we found out."

Another time, Connie went with John to a party hosted by one of his friends who lived in an upscale area of Connecticut. In the middle of the room, a group of about four guys stood jawing about football. John, chatting with the host, noticed Connie, unable to resist a football conversation, sidling up to the group. One of them mentioned an incorrect piece of information.

"No," she piped up.

Four heads whipped around in disbelief.

"No," she explained, "you're wrong. He ran *this* time on grass."

John and his host watched as the group of men—convinced they knew so much about football—listened to this girl earnestly rattling off fact after fact about the player they'd been discussing. Their shoulders began to slump in defeat. John was thoroughly amused.

But even with their mutual adoration, the couple hit another rough patch that January and broke up one last time. Yet John discovered he couldn't escape memories of her—he'd turn on the TV, and some Jets-related story would come on. Jets, Jets, Jets—it was all he seemed to hear.

That breakup proved the shortest: it lasted only three weeks. Near the end of January, Connie and John met up at the restaurant where they had their first date, a place on Long Island called Seascape, and officially got back together. On April 1, he proposed.

Connie wasn't sure he was serious. John's habit of practical jokes, combined with it being April Fool's Day, proved too much of a coincidence for her to feel comfortable, so she made him propose again the next day.

He obliged and agreed later that week that they could tell her parents they were making plans.

Dr. Cal and Lynne, when they found out, raised no objection. They had made a pact long ago that if their child truly loved someone, they would never create obstacles to the union. Their attitude had grown from the drama of their own difficult courtship, back when they first met as undergrads at Cornell in the 1940s. Both had taken circuitous routes there—Lynne had attended an all-girls college for two years, while Calvin had transferred from Fordham. Calvin, for as brilliant as he was, had been a late bloomer academically—he'd worked at least forty hours a week since he was 12 years old and cared more about playing baseball than anything else (including girls). In fact, his high school grades were so low that it took a priest's intercession to get him into Fordham University in 1941. At first, he worked as an elevator attendant to earn his way through college, holding the door for passengers or guiding them to the correct floor, appreciative of the tips he received. The experience taught him to always be generous when tipping someone. He eventually joined the Navy, which sent him to Cornell for a year as part of its V-12 program. One day, he boarded a train and spotted a beautiful girl up ahead of him. He noticed her golden hair first and was eventually so mesmerized by her that he got up, left his seat and the buddy he'd been traveling with, and approached her. He wanted the seat next to hers, but one of her friends already occupied it. Calvin persuaded the friend to move, and he sat down. And then he and Lynne talked. And talked. She'd grown up in a poor Polish family. He was the son of Greek immigrants. She loved to dance and had a soft spot for baseball, which he played. He'd never had a girlfriend. She'd had plenty of suitors, but he must have stacked up well against them—when the railcar stopped, he'd earned a kiss. By the end of the ride, they were smitten.

But they had forgotten someone.

Julia Nicholas, when she discovered the object of her son's new romance, was incensed. Lynne might be the ideal bride for someone else—she was stunning, educated, kind-hearted, and an undeniable lady, who never set foot in a bar and always dressed modestly—but she would not do for Julia Nicholas's son, for a reason beyond the young woman's control: she wasn't Greek. Because of that, Julia absolutely refused to accept her. But her son stood firm—he refused to change his mind or his choice.

So Julia began scheming. No detail was too miniscule to be useless. She invited the couple over to her house and cooked the most outlandish dishes, hoping somehow they would scare Lynne off. She stalled the couple's relationship through Calvin's graduation in 1945 and acceptance into medical school. Finally, she marched to the dean at the medical school and insisted he flunk her son unless he gave up Lynne. By now, Lynne had begun losing weight under the stress—over the five-year war Julia waged against them, the young woman shrunk from 158 to 110 pounds. But she stayed by Cal's side.

In the end, they won. It was Julia Nicholas who caved, her iron will bent by a force even more powerful. Maybe she finally realized Calvin wasn't going to change his mind; perhaps she'd privately decided Lynne deserved a chance. Lynne's father, Dziadzie, also paid Julia a visit and reasoned she needed to accept the young couple's relationship. Julia had great respect for Dziadzie—though lovable, he was a strong businessman; in fact, he was probably the only man Julia ever really feared. The couple ultimately married in 1948 with her blessing, and Julia quickly came to adore her new daughter. What's more, Lynne never held a grudge against her mother-in-law for the misery she'd caused and often softened her husband towards his intractable parent. But the experience had molded the couple's attitude toward their own children; never, if they could help it, would Chris, Connie, or Bruce be forced to suffer as they had. And so they welcomed John Carberg—whom they loved anyway—with open arms, and the happy couple was soon working on wedding plans for the upcoming year.

Part III: Validation

I learned as much about dealing with people from Connie as she learned from me.

— RECOMMENDATION LETTER FROM MIKE HICKEY
FORMER DIRECTOR OF PLAYER PERSONNEL
NEW YORK JETS

CHAPTER 13

Penalized

As Connie and John were falling in love, major changes were taking place within the Jets.

Holtz's departure that December of 1976 had left the franchise once again searching for a new head coach. Within a few days, the Jets settled on an internal candidate: Walt Michaels, the team's defensive coordinator and Nicholas family friend. The team admitted later they never really spoke to another person about the job, though the hire wasn't confirmed publicly till the following month.[i] Connie was overjoyed with the hire; she fondly remembered the mastermind of the Super Bowl III defense swinging by her parents' house and teaching her about football as they watched games with her family. Since her beloved Holtz had to leave, Michaels was a thrilling successor.

But the death of Jets owner Phil Iselin, who passed away not long after the medical episode in Denver, had also left a vacancy at the organization's top. Into that void stepped Leon Hess, voted acting president of the franchise the same week the Jets announced Michaels's contract in January of 1977.

If Hess had once appeared hands-off on football operations, that attitude had now changed. He had been with the franchise almost since its inception as part of the cadre of men who had joined with Sonny Werblin in 1963 to purchase the team. Though Werblin had sold his interest the offseason before the Super Bowl victory, Hess and the other families stayed on, through the Super Bowl triumph and subsequent demise, and it was now his job to usher the team into a new era.

For it was destined to be a new era, whether the Jets desired it or not. That year, for the first time in over a decade, Joe Namath would not take the field in a Jets uniform. Age had done its work; as his contract option came up that offseason, the team appeared to feel it could no longer justify the paycheck to its franchise quarterback, who was battling as best he could on rickety knees and through back pain.[ii] The two sides parted, and Namath ultimately signed with the Los Angeles Rams. Even as a Jet, his star power had exerted influence on the West Coast; during one trip to San Diego, a young boy had approached him at a restaurant.

"My father says you're the best quarterback to ever play football," the boy told him.

Namath, as usual, asked the kid's name before signing an autograph. But then he did something else. At another table, the quarterback of the San Diego Chargers was out to dinner with his offensive line.

"You see who that is?" Namath asked the boy. "You're from San Diego. You see that table over there?

That's Dan Fouts and his offensive lineman. Go over there. Dan's the greatest quarterback playing today. Go over and get his autograph."

It did not follow, however, that even when Namath relocated to California, a part of his heart would not remain with the team and town that had drafted him, celebrated him, criticized and loved him for twelve seasons. While chatting with a *Newsday* reporter and praising his new situation, from the enviable weather to the people around him, Namath was also honest about what New York still meant to him. "I miss New York, friends I have there," he said. "I miss the Jets. I love the Jets. I miss people like Bill Hampton and Connie Nicholas and so many others with that team. I miss players, and Leon Hess, who was so good to me. Hell, I don't have any complaints. This is a great life."[iii]

Namath's departure may have been the most public change the Jets sustained that year, but there were others deep at work in the organization. Leon Hess had several items he wanted to implement moving forward, and one of them directly concerned Connie. Hess was born of a different era, one where women had made fewer inroads into the brave new world of untraditional roles they began filling as the decades progressed. Even now, the idea of a woman boss, or a woman receiving a scholarship to play sports in college, was still a relatively fresh concept. And when Hess had to decide what a woman should be allowed to do in his organization, the answer was not going out to college teams to scout players. He didn't appear to doubt Connie's capabilities, but the public act, the presentation of a woman as a representative of the Jets scouting department, seemed unable to find a place in his view for the franchise.

Ward got wind of what was coming. When Hess showed up at the Hofstra complex to meet with him, the general manager tried to argue on Connie's behalf. He could argue very little, however; Hess was a complete boss, and Ward knew excess words on the subject would be futile. The owner had made up his mind that Connie was no longer permitted to travel as a scout. Nothing else would change; she could still grade film and file reports and carry on with whatever other scouting assignments she picked up at the office. But travel, such as she had done to Ohio State and the Orange Bowl, was forbidden.

It was a difficult moment for the general manager as he carried the verdict to his unsuspecting employee. Ward knew what Connie's work meant to her. He'd helped nurture her career; now, he felt it would nearly crush her to hear the news he must deliver. He relayed the new development: all of her duties would remain intact, but she could no longer travel on scouting assignments.

Connie was blindsided. At work, she had always refused to see gender as the enemy. Men, in fact, had been her greatest allies: visionaries like Woody Hayes, Mike Holovak, and Ward himself had supported her, mentored her, believed in her, and always made her feel an equal. And for this to come from Mr. Hess, who had known her family for years and witnessed her passion and love for the organization! For the first time in her career, her hard work had failed to overcome whatever preconceived prejudice someone brought against her because she was a woman.

But in the moment, an emotion that lay even deeper than disappointment rose up to guide her—an unflinching loyalty to this organization, which had been with her since childhood and given her so much. One unfair decision could not erase years of love and memories. In a roundabout way, she and Hess were one and the same: they would both do whatever they thought best for their organization. Raising a fuss that would damage the Jets was her greatest worry. To be stripped of a privilege, she could tolerate. To be separated from the Jets was unthinkable.

And so she conveyed to the general manager that she understood. Ward, in fact, thought she took the news well. Privately, a few family members saw her deep disappointment—her brother Chris, and, of course, John. But her old habit of cultivating optimism, the example her parents set of never holding grudges, served her well now. She returned to her work with no thought of revenge or souring of attitude. Connie had always operated by building bridges, not burning them. She wasn't going to start now.

Perhaps, if Mike Holovak had stayed with the team, things might have been different. But Holovak, too, had left the Jets that year. After serving as interim coach for the final game in '76 after Holtz resigned, he'd been passed over for the head coaching job and chose to depart after the draft in May, leaving behind a heartbroken young personnel assistant and one of the top draft classes the team ever assembled.[iv] In his place, the team hired a young man named Mike Hickey, who'd worked as a scout and assistant personnel director with the New England Patriots.

When Hickey arrived, the contrast in style and substance with the man he replaced could not have been more obvious. Holovak had been unassuming, keenly perceptive, and quietly sure of himself. At 30 years old, Hickey was a loud, physically imposing specimen, the kind that filled the hallway when he stood in it. His last name was synonymous with football ingenuity because of his father, Red Hickey, a legend for inventing the sport's widely used shotgun formation. Perhaps Hickey felt pressure to prove he'd inherited some of his father's creative genius; he took IQ tests for fun and strained hard at work to discover diamonds in the rough others had overlooked. One year, he was ecstatic about a first-round pick the Jets were going to make that many would have viewed as a startling selection at that point in the draft. Hickey, who guarded draft secrets with a conscientiousness that bordered on paranoia, had even kept the public relations department in the dark.

"I can't wait to see the look on [PR director Frank Ramos's] face tomorrow when we take [this player] in the first round," he confided to then-team president Jim Kensil.

Kensil, however, foresaw an impending public relations disaster.

"Mike, that's not going to happen, because you're going to tell Frank," Kensil insisted. "What I don't want is to have the television cameras on Frank, and Frank having a surprised look on his face, or a look—possibly—of disappointment on his face. I want Frank to be very up about this when he hears this, and you're going to tell him the reasons we're taking [this guy]."

Hickey relented, and Ramos, duly warned, played up the pick appropriately when the announcement was made.

Meanwhile, a curveball that awaited Hickey as he assumed his new job was the unusual young woman working in his scouting department. Unlike others in the organization, he had no point of reference for who Connie was or what she knew; he hadn't witnessed her football obsession from childhood on, or everything she'd accomplished since joining the franchise. Connie understood instinctively that if she wanted her new boss's respect, she would have to earn it—and it wouldn't be easy.

He started by telling her that he didn't think she should be able to attend Jets practice anymore. This, to Connie, was a blow more terrible than being banned from scouting trips. During her time with the Jets, no one had ever bothered her about her ritual of observing practice; they hadn't cared, as long as her other work was completed on time, and she had always made sure it was. She also felt being able to observe practice was key to her work evaluating players.

Upset, she discussed the dilemma with John. In general, John proved an effective resource in her ongoing battles with Hickey—he'd given so many sales and motivational seminars for work that he could rattle off effective techniques on working with people in a professional setting. When trying to close a deal, he once told her, put out a statement and then be quiet. Don't keep talking. If a person keeps talking, the other person usually realizes their opponent is nervous and gains the advantage. The first one to speak after a deal was presented usually lost.

Armed with John's encouragement, Connie felt emboldened to stand up for herself. Nervous but determined, she broached the issue with Hickey.

"In the past," she explained to him, "I always went to practice."

"There's no reason, really, for you to have to go to practice," Hickey observed. "You're in here doing your work."

But Connie stood firm.

"Really, for me to be able to judge players and watch what's going on, that needs to be part of my work," she insisted. "I've always watched practice. I've grown up with this. To continue learning, to keep watching, to be able to see how the players are progressing, to know what's happening out on the field, to be able to interview the players, to be able to grade films, I need to be able to be out on the practice field. That is part of my job."

To his credit, Hickey, after hearing her out, came around.

"I think you're right," he agreed.

She had closed the deal and secured her objective, but the incident was far from a silver bullet to winning Hickey's trust. If this was a battle for respect, it was one she would have to win by doing a million little things right.

It helped having Walt Michaels in charge of the coaching department. Hickey had due deference for

Michaels's genius, and the coach, in turn, had great respect for Connie's opinion. Sometimes, Michaels called her downstairs to his office—when the Jets had added a second story to the Hofstra complex, she'd been given her own small office at the top of the steps—and requested her help.

"Connie, I need you to find something out for me," he'd say, and ask for information on college prospects for the upcoming draft.

That offseason, there was an undersized player at the small, out-of-the-way college Michaels's son attended who desperately wanted a tryout with the Jets. At approximately 5'8" and 176 pounds, Kutztown State running back Bruce Harper would likely be too small to play his position in the pros, but his final season at Kutztown State, he kept asking Michaels's son if he'd be willing to call his dad and see if Harper could get a tryout. Harper felt he'd asked a million times before the younger Michaels finally agreed. His dad appeared to listen, however, for Harper—who went undrafted that May—made the Jets' free agent list and received an invitation to camp that summer.

But when the running back, accompanied by his former coach (who'd served as his agent with the Jets), arrived at the complex for the start of camp, his new surroundings had him feeling like a fish out of water.[v] Here he was, a no-name kid who'd had to scrap and beg for an invitation, at a real pro football organization, trying to compete against guys drafted from some of the country's most prestigious collegiate programs. As he walked into the building, he was feeling very unsure of himself. But when he said his name,

Connie recognized him immediately. She greeted him with a smile and was so warm and personable that Harper was blown away.

Is this for real? Harper thought. *Is the whole organization like this?*

Her friendliness began to put him at ease. Later, when he and the other camp attendees gathered for their first day of work on the field, he looked around for someone who might be willing to help him stretch for the 40-yard dash. He settled on a guy with a majestic Afro.

"Come here, man, help me out," Harper begged him.

The stranger obliged. Harper got up and ran his 40. Then the player who'd been helping him got up and ran *his* 40. Harper was stunned—it was arguably the fastest 40 he'd ever seen in his life. He later discovered the player he'd accosted was the team's second-round draft pick, wide receiver Wesley Walker.

Walker's assist must have been golden, however, for Harper, whose confidence came soaring back when he stepped onto the football field, made the team that season, primarily for his contributions on special teams. He was ultimately too small to withstand the beating of an every-down running back, but the Jets eventually pioneered him in the role of a third-down back, used mainly in clutch times when the team needed the extra yardage. Harper's speed and shiftiness made him particularly suited for that role, but so did his attitude—if he couldn't get around someone, he would try his hardest to run right over them. Harper was always willing to put his head down and go for whatever yards his team needed.

As for Walker, he may have been able to empathize more with Harper's journey to the pros than the young back realized. He, too, had overcome a significant physical drawback to wear an NFL uniform, for he'd been born legally blind in his left eye. He was painfully self-conscious of it, for the eye would drift and make him appear cross-eyed. People poked fun at him, but he'd generally tried to avoid mentioning his condition growing up, fearing it could take away his chance to play sports. In high school and college, people were vaguely aware of the handicap, but Walker's performance always rendered it a non-issue, so much that the Jets never seemed to have an inkling of it before the draft. They were worried instead about Walker's knee, which he'd injured in college and had undergone surgery to repair. Before drafting him, the Jets sent a trainer out to evaluate Walker, whose knee passed muster. But when he showed up at Jets camp after the draft and underwent a full physical examination, the team was shocked to discover their newest wide receiver was blind in one eye. And it wasn't the only medical issue the team learned they'd missed that year—their first-round draft pick, big tackle Marvin Powell out of USC, had a loose knee.

Leon Hess, when he found out, was livid. He was sitting at a big, round table with the medical personnel, wrapping up the results of the examinations, when the ophthalmologist spoke up.

"One guy's blind in one eye."

"Who?"

"Wesley Walker."

Even Dr. Jim looked stunned. Hess almost choked on his cigar.

"You mean to tell me," he said, "*that our No. 1 and No. 2 picks have injuries that might prevent them from playing in the NFL*?"

He didn't know at the time, of course, that both cases would turn out well—Walker became one of the best receivers in Jets history, and Powell reached five Pro Bowls. But what if, next time, things didn't work out? Athletes themselves couldn't be trusted when it came to injuries, for they were usually determined to play at all costs. Dr. Cal saw it dozens of times with young players. During summer camp in 1968, a rookie defensive back named John Dockery had suffered a leg injury that hampered him from running or pushing himself to his utmost capability. The only cure for his injury, Dr. Cal informed him, was a combination of physical therapy and rest. But Dockery objected.

"I have to practice," he told Dr. Cal. "If I don't, I'll never have a chance."

Dr. Cal answered as he always did.

"If they're interested in you from what you've shown so far, they *will* wait," he insisted. "If not, you'll be cut anyway. And if you practice and do lousy, you'll be cut just the same."

Dockery ultimately waited, returned, and won the Super Bowl with the Jets that year.

But there was no reason, Hess believed, that if a player had an injury *prior* to the draft, the Jets shouldn't know about it and decide accordingly. The league itself had no uniform process to determine a player's physical fitness before being drafted (an injury might merit a brief mention in a scouting report, but the scout himself wasn't equipped to provide medical analysis). If the Jets wanted things to change, *they* would have to be the catalyst and radically revamp their own protocol before the next draft.

They decided to fly the top hundred or so prospects into New York after the college football season was over and have them undergo a *thorough* pre-draft physical at Lenox Hill Hospital. It would also be a chance to talk with the athletes, as one would in a job interview, and get a better feel for their character and whether they liked playing in New York. What the Jets gathered could be combined with the traditional scouting reports to offer a more detailed picture. It was a vast undertaking—they were looking at arranging the travel of at least a hundred young men from different areas of the country and having them arrive during the brief window of time when the medical personnel would be set up to examine them in New York. But first, they had to track each player down.

That, they soon discovered, proved difficult. The team was operating on a constricted timeline between the end of football season and the draft, which meant they needed to locate players quickly. The process became an all-hands-on-deck collaboration between the training staff and the scouting department, and Connie and her coworkers found themselves stretching in creative ways to get the job done. The only personal information they usually had on a player was his name and school. They had to call the school—the head secretary at the football office was a key contact—and, since the football season was already over, it was often a gamble on where to go next; they could try their luck with an apartment phone or dorm phone (which might be a pay phone in the middle of a dormitory) and hope, if the player wasn't in, that he'd call back. Another option was calling the athletic director to see if he could deliver the message. A Jets trainer once found himself calling a local sheriff's department while trying to track down a draft-eligible player who'd flashed star potential but quit school and had a trail of disconnected telephone numbers in his wake.

In all this, Connie proved invaluable. She was tenacious on assignment, determined to find her man no matter how many people she had to call. Jets trainers sometimes called their counterparts at college programs and asked them to pass a message on to a desired player; Connie discovered another method was to contact one of the player's more readily accessible teammates whom the Jets had already scheduled to bring in and get *him* to relay the message. Her successes, she felt, helped prove her worth to Hickey, who witnessed them firsthand.

In fact, when the players finally arrived in New York, she was one of the people chosen to interview them. She essentially just tried to have a good conversation with each player, which allowed her to glean an idea of their character and motivation through simple interview questions: why they chose the college they went to, what they hoped to be in the pros, what football meant to them, what they thought of New York. She might ask if they played other sports, which suggested strong athletic ability. Everything boiled down to a few key points: was football the most important thing to them? If they'd gone to a prestigious academic school like Stanford or Notre Dame, they clearly had other career options—would they be as hungry as someone who considered football their only way to success? Did they seem coachable? Could they be happy in New York? Some players would just come out and say they weren't really looking to be in a big city, or were scared of it. Others indicated it was no issue.

All told, in the spring of 1978, the Jets brought in 105 athletes; four other players, unable to make the trip, were examined at major colleges. The pioneering endeavor did not go unnoticed outside the Jets facility; an assistant trainer with the Buffalo Bills told one member of the Jets training staff that the whole concept was ridiculous. The Jets, however, found it so productive that they brought in nearly 200 players the following year. As more and more teams caught on, players found themselves swamped with invitations. Even in general, before the '79 draft, eventual first-round picks Barry Krauss and Marty Lyons, who played together at the University of Alabama, visited so many teams that they basically had to drop out of school the latter part of their senior year. When Alabama head coach Bear Bryant found out, he was so upset that he called them in and chewed them out for missing so many classes. They needed to finish their education, he insisted.

But the players didn't know what else to do. They had few, if any, places to turn for advice on the logistics of transitioning to the pros; in fact, when Krauss went to Bryant and asked him to recommend an agent, Bryant refused to, perhaps concerned about the validity of an agent to recommend. Krauss finally got one just before the draft, only to discover the agent had no clue what he was doing; he orchestrated a long-term deal for Krauss and then, the player felt, essentially vanished. When Krauss found out what his peers were negotiating for, he was stunned at how poorly his own contract compared. There had been no way to educate himself on the process, either; the NFL didn't give out information on player salaries, so Krauss had no idea what he should be commanding heading into negotiations.

That didn't mean the teams themselves were always organized during the draft process, either, as Krauss discovered when the Tampa Bay Buccaneers brought him, Lyons, and another teammate, Tony Nathan, down for a visit. That night in Tampa, the players enjoyed a nice dinner that added several hundred dollars to their tab; the next day, they discovered the hotel had neglected to inform them of their per diem allocation from the team, an amount far closer to $50 than several hundred. In fact, when Nathan went to get his luggage out of his hotel room before the trio left Tampa, he found the door locked against him.

Perplexed, the players went to the front office.

"We can't get in," they explained. "Tony needs to get his luggage—we're leaving."

"I'm sorry," the hotel employee told them. "The general manager of the Tampa Bay Buccaneers isn't allowing you to leave until you pay your tab."

The general manager, when appealed to, quickly began yelling about the trio's expensive dinner.

"You pay your bill and then get the heck out of here," he snapped. "We're not drafting you."

"We don't want to come here, either," came the response. Luckily, Nathan had a credit card, so the trio put the dinner amount on that, retrieved his ransomed bags, and left.

Eventually, players' visits to different NFL teams grew so voluminous that a national scouting service—to which sixteen teams around the league subscribed—held one camp before the draft where players could come for physicals, with the results shared among those sixteen teams. Two other national scouting services followed suit, and soon the entire league agreed to take part in one consolidated event, which became known as the NFL Scouting Combine.[vi]

At home, meanwhile, Connie and John were in the throes of wedding planning. They'd started out with a list of about 250 guests, but then they sat down together one night and admitted they were inviting some people they hardly knew or frankly weren't fond of. They decided they only wanted people around them that day who made them truly happy, so that whoever they spotted when they turned around to look at the assembled guests, they would feel joy at seeing them present. The list was pared to around 80 invitees; a date was selected for the following spring: May of 1979.

Not long after the date was set, Connie approached Hickey to let him know she'd be taking time off the following May for her wedding.

"No, you can't," Hickey responded.

Connie was startled.

"Why?" she wanted to know.

"You only have off in June," he told her. June was a notoriously slow month on the NFL calendar; it fell conveniently between the draft and the start of summer camp, so many team employees scheduled time off during that stretch.

"But we want to get married in May," Connie argued.

"No, you can't do that," Hickey decided.

Connie went home and told John what had happened. John thought it was ridiculous and said she should confront Hickey. Once again, Connie went back to her boss. The wedding, she informed him, would be in May.

"You can't say when I get married," she said firmly. "That's the date that I'm going to be married, no matter what, and you have to live with that."

Hickey relented.

In the end, however, she and John got married in neither May nor June. When they talked with her parents, Dr. Cal and Lynne asked why the couple had chosen a date so far off. They were in love—why wait? Ultimately, Connie and John agreed, and Connie decided to move their wedding up to a weekend in late January. Only later did she realize the date she'd chosen was Super Bowl weekend.

But she was so in love, she didn't care.

CHAPTER 14

The Discovery

Connie sifted through the materials at hand, looking for an answer.

How could she find something countless eyes had missed?

College football players were some of the most scrutinized people in the country. She was being asked to find a diamond in the rough, someone who'd been overlooked, who could fill in on one of the biggest stages in college football.

The clock was ticking.

It had begun with a call from Hickey. He used to ring her office phone at 1:00 p.m. every day when he was on the road; likely, Connie realized, to make sure her lunch break hadn't extended too long. She was always there, so eventually, he'd stopped.

This call wasn't routine, though—it was urgent. Mike Stensrud, a premiere defensive lineman from Iowa State, had been scheduled to play in the upcoming Senior Bowl on January 13, 1979. The game functioned as a red carpet event to the NFL draft, and college seniors invited to the bowl were divided into two teams, the North and South. The Jets were in charge of coaching the North that year, with Stensrud slotted as a defensive end. But that past Saturday, Stensrud, leaving a bar, missed a turn while driving his snowmobile and opted to cut through a nearby field rather than return to the road. Flying between 45-50 miles an hour, he careened into a ditch and was knocked unconscious. When the group he'd been out with earlier came looking for him, they found him lying at the bottom of the ditch, his snowmobile smashed. He didn't remember much of what had happened and realized within 48 hours he wouldn't be able to play in the upcoming Senior Bowl. The Jets needed a replacement—fast.

Connie hung up the phone.[i] She was being entrusted—under an extremely tight deadline—with finding a substitute for a guy who'd repeated as an All-American and Big Eight defensive tackle that year, in addition to garnering Hula and Senior Bowl invites. In fact, on the eve of Stensrud's senior season, an Iowa State assistant coach had speculated Stensrud "could be the best ever to wear this uniform."[ii]

She'd worked through several candidates with what information she had: reel-to-reel film, whatever the Jets had on hand, since there wasn't enough time to request copies from the schools, and the scouting reports, which tried to capture a guy's entire playing style, physical attributes, and intangibles via the numerical grading system and several dry, Spartan sentence fragments, just like she herself often wrote. Then again, *if you need a dissertation to explain why a guy can play,* one scout later observed, *you don't know the player.*

The problem was, after all her scrutiny, this handful of defensive ends seemed fairly equal. One contender was a first-team All-American. Another, Mark Gastineau, had good speed, she noted. But he went to a smaller school than some others in the group—East Central Oklahoma, where he'd transferred after playing in the vastly more prestigious Arizona State program. He would likely be only a sixth- or seventh-rounder in the upcoming draft.[iii] Still, she'd been trained by men who believed a player's most important trait wasn't always measurable. Mike Holovak had always cared less about size and weight and speed than the answer to a simple question: *can the guy play football?*

But with this group, she had no time for in-person observation. She wouldn't have been allowed to go, anyway—Leon Hess's edict had seen to that.

An idea struck her. She'd never tried it before while scouting, but it was the only option the ticking clock allowed. She'd call the players, see if she could glean something through conversation—and hope she could reach them in time.

She began dialing each one, explaining there was a possibility he could play in the Senior Bowl. What she offered was arguably the chance of a lifetime—a shot at playing for actual NFL coaches on a high-profile stage.

She was stunned by what struck her as laissez-faire reception. In general, the players' responses seemed, at least to her ears, tepid—they wanted more details, sounded unsure of what the Senior Bowl was, or thought they needed to get in better shape. Connie felt instinctively something was missing: desire.

The next guy on the list was Mark Gastineau. Connie began punching the numbers on the base of the phone and waited.

Mark always remembered the first time he started believing in God—or, at least, believed there *was* a God.

He'd been born in wind-swept Oklahoma—a child of the West and its fiery, unbridled spirit. When he was 10, he'd tried scaling a fence to recover a volleyball his sister had lost, but his leg caught between two bars. His mother—who'd warned him against climbing the fence—pulled him out and brought him inside, but the damage was already done: his leg was broken. Then doctors put the cast on too tight, and he almost got gangrene. When the cast was removed, there was a hole in the side of his leg, deep to the bone. Ligaments were gone.

Mark was frightened. Blood and puss oozed all over the hospital table from his limb. When he looked down, he could see the table through the hole in his leg. His mom almost passed out. The young boy was told he would never walk again.

But his mom had been going to a Baptist church, a small congregation of around 35 members.

"The church is praying for you," she told her son. "You'll walk."

Mark believed her. Sitting in the hospital bed, he, too, began praying for help. Within a couple of years, the leg had healed, and he'd learned to walk and run again—well enough, in fact, to play high school football at his new home in Springerville, Arizona. After attending junior college and being named an All-American, he moved to the illustrious football program at Arizona State on scholarship.

The new campus was huge, maybe twice the size of Mark's hometown. In the midst of masses, he began to feel achingly lonely. He started smoking pot with some of his teammates and grew lazy. He also disliked head coach Frank Kush's abrasive coaching style and blew off a game. Finally, Mark admitted he needed to leave.

Kush, when he realized a scholarship player was about to walk out the door, was furious. Along with an overdose of name-calling, the coach told Mark he would never play professional football.

"You will never, *ever,* get drafted if you leave this school," Kush ranted. "If you think that you're going to play in the NFL, your chances are none."

Mark left anyway—and was glad about it.

Uncertain of his next step, he went on a road trip with his father to look at another school, and on the way back, they swung by a town called Ada, home to tiny East Central Oklahoma. Mark loved the school's size, and the school loved his—they couldn't believe an athlete with his broad, 6'5" frame was walking through their doors saying he wanted to play for their football program. "Big Daddy," they called him.

They gave him the best of what they had, which wasn't much. At Arizona State, the equipment was pristine; players sported brand new socks and shiny new headgear. At East Central, there was no budget for such luxuries. The jocks looked like they were from the 1930s. Things smelled of mildew. The weight room resembled a dungeon.

But at last, Mark was happy. He worked endlessly on his speed, desperate to give himself an edge that would entice NFL scouts to his small school. He began running 40-yard dashes and figured out when he practiced downhill, he ran faster—his body was forced to speed up to keep him from falling. On the campus, there was a long cement slab sloping down toward a dam; at night, sometimes under a streetlight's supervision, Mark kept running.

It paid off. When football great Mel Renfro, working with a national scouting service, first timed Mark in the 40-yard dash, the stellar results made Renfro think his watch malfunctioned.

"This is broke," Renfro said, referring to his watch.

"Why is it broke?"

"It says 4.5. And the time before, it was like 4.6. So it's not working right."

“No, no, no, no, it's working right!” Mark exclaimed.

Renfro got another stopwatch anyway and made Mark run two more dashes, just to be sure.

When Connie reached Mark that winter, he was back in Springerville, steadfastly refusing to go skiing in the nearby White Mountains during his stay, worried a ski injury might make him unable to train for football. The college football season was essentially over, but Mark thought he might be able to squeak into the NFL as a 12th-round draft pick, and he wanted to be ready, just in case.

When Connie got him on the phone, the young man's passion swept through the line like a gale through a palm tree.

"Just tell me anywhere to be, just let me know where to go," he insisted. *I'm ready to go right now,* his attitude shouted.

He was so different from the others. She could hear heart in his voice—raw, unbridled enthusiasm that stirred the depths of her scouting instincts. This, she knew, was her guy.

On Monday, five days before the Senior Bowl, the Jets announced Mark Gastineau would be replacing the injured Stensrud on the North squad. Unbeknownst to the young athlete, on his shoulders rested the ultimate validation of a young woman's pioneering career. His play would prove whether her insight and acumen, culled over years of study from the moment she first ventured into Paul Albert's classroom as a bright-eyed, spunky 12-year-old, could stand up to the most secretive, male-dominated clique in professional sports.

With no work reason to travel to Mobile, Alabama, for the Senior Bowl, and her wedding just one week away, Connie remained in New York as scouts and players crowded into the Deep South for the event. The bowl itself could attract crowds of around 40,000. Each of the 66 players from the previous year's Senior Bowl, with only four exceptions, had been drafted into the NFL.[iv] The event was a boon for the head coach of each squad, too; they would get significant time working with the nation's top seniors, a way to glean valuable insight with a draft only a few months away.

In Mobile, Mark was turning heads. His first day at practice, he blazed by players from marquee schools. After his second day of practice, he discovered the phone in his hotel had rung incessantly. The front desk handed him a huge stack of papers: hundreds of messages from agents interested in making him a client.

Mark brought the papers to his room, which he shared with another defensive lineman, burley Fred Smerlas from Boston College.

"Fred, can you believe this?" he asked.

"It's because of how you practice," Smerlas responded, then asked incredulously, as if he, too, couldn't quite fathom where this unheralded force of a talent had sprung from, "*Where* you from?"

By Friday of that week, Jets head coach Walt Michaels told the press that Mark had been the biggest surprise in practice.

On game day, he didn't disappoint. Though the Jets-coached North lost by 20 points, Mark Gastineau, from tiny East Central Oklahoma, dominated enough to be named the team's top defensive lineman. Connie watched his thrilling performance via television broadcast, relieved to replace the pressure of her assignment with warm pride in the young man's accomplishment.

In fact, Mark's performance had created a spotlight big enough to illuminate even his towering frame and surreal speed, skyrocketing his stock among NFL teams. Pro scouts flocked to him. Marv Sunderland, hired by the Jets scouting department that February, worked him out and became a fan. Chuck Knox, the Buffalo Bills head coach, flew into Ada on a Learjet. The Bills even brought him in for a pre-draft physical. At some point, accepted parlance from some scouts became how they'd discovered Mark *at* the Senior Bowl; apparently, no one stopped to wonder *how* he'd gotten there.[v]

Back in New York, Connie quietly began her predraft preparation for the Jets. It would've been odd, if she'd stopped to think about it—she'd changed the young man's life, and yet they'd never actually met. While Mark visited with agents, she continued in cheerful obscurity at the Jets' facilities, her role in his newfound stardom unknown even to most of the organization. Nor did she expect, or look for it—a scout didn't chase notoriety or public accolades. The NFL draft that year was in May, four months after the Senior Bowl. There was work to do.

By five or six in the morning on May 3, Jets personnel were at the team's Long Island complex, set for a marathon draft day that usually ended around nine or ten in the evening. Walt Michaels and Hickey were part of the group camped in the Jets' "war room," now located on the second floor of the complex. Inside the room were boards featuring columns of cards detailing pertinent player information: name, school, height, weight, Wonderlic test score,[1] scouting grade assigned by the Jets, speed in the 40-yard dash and whether it had been run on grass or Astroturf, since players ran faster on turf. The top players also had a rating according to the results of their pre-draft physicals—from "High Priority," or HP, which meant they'd checked out, to P1, P2, P3, flunked, or some combination therein (such as P1/P2). The cards, encased in clear plastic holders, could be rearranged as the day progressed. Connie, who'd spent the past two months helping compile the information on those cards and lining them up on the board in whatever order the football staff needed, was camped at her usual station—a small table in the corner with a telephone—ready to call the team's selections in to Jets personnel at draft headquarters in New York. The Jets' first pick that year was exactly halfway through the first round at number 14. That meant thirteen other teams had a chance to pilfer the player the Jets wanted most on their squad.

---

[1] The Wonderlic was designed to test intelligence.

The Buffalo Bills used the first pick of the entire draft on star linebacker Tom Cousineau, who played at Ohio State. More names followed—quarterback Phil Simms, whom Dr. Jim had failed on his physical with the Jets, went to their archenemy, the New York Giants. Kellen Winslow, a future Hall of Famer, was drafted thirteenth by San Diego, one pick before the Jets went on the clock.

Hickey always moved fast when their turn came—he didn't like taking the full fifteen minutes of decision time afforded each team in the first round. He often preferred to make the first few picks himself, with the Jets scouts not giving input until the later rounds.

The first selection, however, seemed a joint venture between Hickey and Michaels. The team chose heralded prospect Marty Lyons, who reminded Michaels of another defensive lineman he'd once coached—the Nicholases' old family friend, Gerry Philbin. Lyons fit with the Jets' draft plan that year: they wanted players with size, speed, and football intelligence from winning programs. Lyons came from the University of Alabama, a powerhouse program, and had been named top defensive lineman for the South in the Senior Bowl that year. The New York Mets had originally drafted him out of high school to baseball, but he'd chosen to go on a scholarship to Alabama and play football under Bear Bryant.

Connie took the card handed her with Lyons's name. Her daintily manicured hands—she'd taken to wearing red nail polish, like her mother did—dialed the league's location in New York City, and she calmly read off Lyons's name and school, spelling his name to ensure accuracy. The Jets representative on the end of the line repeated the information back, and the conversation finished, so that the pick could be handed to the league commissioner. The selection was official.

With Lyons netted safely at No. 14, the Jets' next scheduled turn wasn't until No. 41. Names kept falling off the board. A familiar one was called at 31—Mike Stensrud, the first defensive player selected in the second round. He was headed to Houston.

The Bills were up next. Connie's brother, Bruce, was now working in the Bills' scouting department; he'd actually been cautioned by his boss, "Don't tell your sister all our secrets." The siblings, for their part, avoided any accidental exchange of either team's draft strategy by not speaking to each other at that time of year. There had been an internal discussion among the Bills on whether to select Mark with their 32nd pick, or the man who'd been his roommate at the Senior Bowl, Fred Smerlas. Smerlas was steady and reliable, while Mark played in peaks and valleys. And though the Bills felt Smerlas could immediately contribute, Mark's long-term potential was tantalizing.

Mark, waiting in Oklahoma, received a call from the Bills.[vi]

We're picking you instead of Smerlas, they told him. The Bills secretary confirmed she was purchasing his plane ticket to Buffalo for the following morning. He was scheduled to leave Oklahoma at 7:15 a.m.

But within ten minutes, someone from the Bills phoned Mark back, apologized, and explained there'd been a mistake.

"I feel like an ass," the person said. "But we drafted Smerlas."

Mark went back to waiting, relieved he'd escaped Buffalo.

Nine picks later—and twenty-seven agonizing slots after selecting Lyons—the Jets were on the clock again. The team had gone for size and speed with their first pick; they planned to do so again. They'd witnessed Mark's performance in Mobile and recognized him as a young talent on the rise. Marv Sunderland, after working him out, had realized he was a superior athlete. Michaels loved him, and Hickey seemed on board. There was no reason to hesitate. Mark Gastineau was becoming a New York Jet.

For the young woman waiting to place the call, elation bubbled to the surface. Connie couldn't contain it—a cheer burst from her lips.

"ALRIGHT!" she yelled triumphantly.

Then she picked up the phone, dialed the Jets personnel waiting at the draft headquarters in New York City, and spoke calmly into the receiver.

"The New York Jets," she said, "select Mark Gastineau, East Central Oklahoma."

This time, there was no retraction. Within two weeks, the young man who'd been told he'd never walk again, and never get drafted, was on his way to New York for a physical with his new team, ready to begin his professional football career.

Connie, meanwhile, back at her desk in the little office upstairs, did not yet know her scouting work that winter had just helped draft one of the greatest players in team history.

CHAPTER 15

A Happier Trail

At some point, Mark and Connie met, though it was uneventful enough that in later years neither remembered when or where. Mark didn't forget, however, that it was her voice he'd heard when the call of a lifetime reached him that day in Arizona—later, he would credit Connie for the opportunity he now enjoyed.

She observed him on the field that year as she stood outside watching practice. The Jets were gradually climbing out of the mire of the mid-1970s; after finishing 3–11 in 1977, they'd improved to 8–8 the next year and were on the way to matching that record in 1979. At one point, their kicker, Pat Leahy, suffered an injury that made it look like punter Chuck Ramsey might have to start for him in an upcoming game against the New England Patriots. Chuck hadn't kicked a field goal or an extra point with the team in months; during his first attempt at practice the day before the game, the ball banged off the right upright and bounced back. On the hill that overlooked the field, Connie stood watching practice, as usual.

"Chuck," one of the coaches said, loudly enough for the whole team to hear. "If you don't feel comfortable doing this, Connie is right here. She'll probably kick for you tomorrow."

Chuck, feeling a bit macho, wasn't exactly keen on spreading the story around. But the joke stuck. After that, any time he would shank a kick in practice or a game, or find himself in a slump, a coach or a player would always come over and say, "I think Connie's inside. We could grab her if you don't feel comfortable kicking anymore today." Eventually, the line became so widespread Chuck and Leahy even started using it on each other. It was all, of course, in good fun, but the comment revealed how those on the field felt about the football IQ of the young woman watching—everyone knew *she* knew her football.

She was also helping train a new hire in the office, a bubbly young lady named Kathy Reade. When Kathy first interviewed with the team, her sister—who'd originally told her of the job opening—indicated the Jets were looking for a woman who was "settled." So Kathy, thinking she probably wouldn't get the job anyway, borrowed her sister's engagement ring and wore it to the interview. She was stunned when the Jets offered her the position and felt terrible she'd faked the engagement. She finally decided to pretend she'd called it off, especially since Connie, with characteristic friendliness, had already started talking about a trousseau (Kathy had no idea what that was). When she eventually confessed the truth to her original boss at the Jets, he reassured her that she could have told him right away; it took several years, however, before she fessed up to Connie, with whom she'd become good friends.

Inside the scouting department, meanwhile, Connie continued as a force to be reckoned with. The following year, the Jets had a scouting position open and brought a guy named Joe Collins to the complex for an interview. Connie was one of the first people he met on arriving, and the two struck up a conversation while Joe waited for Hickey to get out of a meeting. Joe was a little nervous about the interview, but Connie made him feel at home. He'd been scouting for about a year for one of the national services known as BLESTO, a name culled from teams subscribed to its services (such as the Bears, Lions, Eagles, etc). Connie, who also read the player report Joe wrote as part of his interview with the Jets, was soon convinced they needed to hire him—he was eminently likeable, and, she felt, the face the team wanted representing the franchise on the road. She held no grudge that it wouldn't be her; the fact that she fit those qualifications never entered into her analysis. Joe, for his part, really wanted the job, but Connie didn't know that. In fact, worried he wouldn't accept it, she was adamant when she and Hickey discussed the opening.

"What do you think about him?" Hickey asked.

"We have to have him," she insisted. "This is the kind of person that is the representative of the club that you want. You've got to hire him, and he's got to say yes."

Both things came to pass. The Jets offered Joe the job; he accepted it and stayed with the organization through the next sixteen years.

While in town for a few weeks of training camp, he and Connie stood on the sidelines of the practice field together and discussed the players. He was stunned that she knew the Jets playbook. Once, as he stood around with another Jets scout, she observed, "You know, we tried that play against a team last year. And it didn't work then in the red zone, and it's not going to work now. We've got to get rid of that play."

Joe, amazed, glanced over at the other scout.

What the hell? his look said.

The greatest testament to her scouting acumen, however, was the hulking 6'5", 255-pound young man who took the field on weekends and began terrorizing offenses league-wide as the '80s progressed. Playing on a line with Marty Lyons, Joe Klecko, and Abdul Salaam, Mark helped form a defensive unit known as the New York Sack Exchange, whose dominance on the field reinvigorated a beleaguered fan base and brought Shea Stadium to life again. Within a few years, he'd become one of the most prestigious defensive ends in the league. He could hear the opposing team as he lined up: "He's coming over, he's coming over, he's coming over, hey, hey, hey." A habit he'd had all the way back in high school, that of dancing crazily with exuberance after sacking the quarterback, became his trademark on the NFL field and redefined the defensive end position. Others, however, didn't like it. They thought it was showboating. The league finally stepped in before the 1984 season and forbade "prolonged, excessive or premeditated" celebrations, partly because of Mark.[i]

Mark was stunned it had become a big deal. No one had complained about it in high school or college. He viewed the act as merely the outpouring of emotion he'd always displayed—the same passion Connie had detected in that initial phone call and which helped get him the job in the first place.

"Go out there and get a sack and see how happy you are to get back from a double team or a triple team, an offensive back sitting there waiting on you," he explained once several years later. "You'll dance, too."

In 1982, Mark's fourth season with the Jets, the league officially started keeping track of sacks recorded by players in a single season. By the end of the team's 1984 campaign, in a December game against the Tampa Bay Buccaneers, Mark set a record that would remain intact for 17 seasons when he sent Buccaneers quarterback Steve DeBerg to the ground. If anything validated his presence in the NFL, it was the marker he reached in Tampa that December day—22 sacks by one player in a single season.

But by then, Connie was no longer with the Jets.

On January 20, 1979, Connie and John had married in a ceremony at her parents' house. It was a joyful, intimate affair, just as they had hoped. Before the ceremony, the songs that had woven themselves through their dating history played via a recording. Afterwards, they had a full dinner reception at a restaurant in West Islip followed by a low-key honeymoon weekend at the Hilton, where they watched the Pittsburgh Steelers beat the Dallas Cowboys in the Super Bowl (later, they took a more formal honeymoon to Bermuda). Back home, they settled in a tiny, one-bedroom apartment in Mineola on Long Island, blissfully happy.

Their salaries, however, were far from kingly. So John eventually called an excellent sales trainer he knew in Alabama, a man named Joe McGuire, to inquire about other auto jobs in the U.S. He missed Joe the first attempt, but Connie prodded him to call again. Joe ultimately gave John's name to a company in Florida named Southeast Toyota Distributors, who expressed interest. John didn't plan on working for them but agreed with Connie that they should at least go down for the weekend and hear the company's pitch. It proved enticing: the company took the couple out on a 75-foot yacht and offered John double the salary he was making. Still, John was hesitant—the area was so beautiful, the experience so ideal, that he felt they'd spent a weekend in a fantasyland rather than reality.

"Let's just sit on this awhile," he suggested to Connie.

But as they sat onboard the plane for their return flight home, "New York, New York" began playing over the loudspeaker before takeoff. Conscious of the impending decision, both began tearing up. When they got home, they rushed to the television to flip on the Winter Olympics: the Americans were playing the vaunted Russians in hockey. As the clock ticked down, and the score stood 4–3 in the U.S.'s favor, Al Michaels's voice, crescendoing in wonder, challenged the country, "*Do you believe in miracles*?"

But a decision had to be made. Before John left for a seminar in Pennsylvania, he was out driving with Connie and broached the topic again.

"I'll leave it up to you," he told her. He knew what leaving the Jets would mean to her. She'd also recently been invited by Ed Ingles of CBS Radio, who did the halftime interviews on that medium for Jets games, to come on the show and discuss football. It was a huge opportunity, for New York fans still only got Jets or Giants games on the radio and TV broadcasts, which meant the audience for such programming was massive. Connie was also taking voice lessons at the time—there was a rumor that sportscaster Phyllis George might leave NFL Today, and Connie had thought about trying for the spot (though she ultimately decided against it).

But she was also madly in love, young, and naïve; she assumed they would go down to Florida for a few years and eventually return to New York.

"Let's go," she decided.

They began packing and prepping for the upcoming move. John left early for Florida to start working and searching for a place to live; Connie would follow when he found one.

As the days progressed, the consequences of the decision became petrifying. What if Southeast Toyota didn't make good on their offer? She and John were leaving everything—and everyone—they knew and loved. There would be no more draft days, no going to Jets games. She was losing her real family and her Jets family. Before she left, she got several of the players and coaches to sign 8 x 10 personnel photos she could treasure as keepsakes. The organization also threw her a huge going-away party upstairs at the complex, where they gave her a Jets jersey emblazoned with the number "7" for her seven years working for the club. Team president Jim Kensil, Walt Michaels, and even Mike Hickey wrote letters of recommendation. Hickey's showed just how far their relationship had come:

> *During the time she has worked with me, I have found her to be of the highest moral character. She is a vivacious, intelligent, mature, and enthusiastic worker who thrives on challenge, new responsibilities, and blends in a unique ability to never overstep her bounds within the limits of her job description.*
>
> *She is a tireless worker who, in four years, has never looked to make any excuses to escape her responsibility through frustration or illness. I learned as much about dealing with people from Connie as she learned from me.*

> *Mrs. Carberg's insights, work habits, and her intelligence are not confined to the business of football. She certainly would be capable of any type job in the business world whether it be administration, personnel, or public relations. I could not envision any area in which Connie would not be successful. She is an honest, extremely tight-lipped, trusted employee, and is the type of person that you make room for in your organization rather than hope a vacancy will occur.*

Michaels's letter, meanwhile, provided a moving testament to the girl he'd watched grow up:

> *It has been my pleasure to know Connie Nicholas Carberg since 1963. I have observed her through Junior and Senior High School, — always pleasant, always ready to learn, forever helpful . ...*
>
> *Upon graduation from college, she began as a secretary with the New York Jets Football Club. She eventually became specialized in the Scouting Department, directly involved with the evaluation and procurement of prospective professional football players through the annual College Draft.*
>
> *Her willingness to learn and her determination to succeed earned her the title of Talent Scout. She gained the respect and admiration of those in the college and professional ranks because of her total dedication. She will be sad-*

ly missed by the New York Jets Scouting Department.

It wasn't, Connie knew, as if she'd be forever severing ties with the team. Her father still worked there, and surely, she would be back for visits. Still, as she exited on her last day, holding a box in her arms, Connie looked up at the building where she'd started her professional career and cried and cried.

But she'd found something—or someone—she loved even more. The months of separation had been hard on John, too. Sometimes, wracked with longing, he'd go to the hotel where he and Connie had stayed on their visit, park in the lot, and cry. As Connie settled into her seat on the plane bound for Florida, she knew in her heart she'd made the right choice. The person awaiting her at the journey's end was worth any sacrifice. Her entire career had been motivated by love—of a sport, of those who played and coached it, love for those to whom it meant so much. So, too, was her decision to leave.

As the Eastern Airlines jet prepared for takeoff, "New York, New York" once again came onto the loud speaker. Connie's brown eyes brimmed with tears. But she wouldn't be alone much longer.

John was waiting for her. And that was all she needed.

Epilogue

When You're a Jet, You're a Jet All Your Life

It was a rough transition, at first, to life in Florida.

When Connie landed in Ft. Lauderdale, John was there to greet her. Before heading home, they stopped at a restaurant called the Golden Spike Buffet and gorged—likely, she later realized, out of total anxiety. And there was a fresh source for unhappiness as the days passed. John, knowing nothing of the area, had secured a condo for them in a senior community where none of their neighbors were under 50. Connie found it horribly lonely when John was away giving seminars; she sat and cried and listened to Barry Manilow's "I Made It Through the Rain."

The upcoming NFL draft, meanwhile, was scheduled for April and being televised for only the second time in the league's history. Connie, dying to watch it, drove all along the beach, trying to find a hotel with cable. When she finally found one, she rented a room and called the Jets to let them know where she was. The team was scheduled to pick third that year; after linebacker Lawrence Taylor went second to the Giants, Jets team president Jim Kensil called Connie.

"We know how important this is to you," he said. "We're going to select Freeman McNeil." McNeil was a running back out of UCLA.

Connie was touched. She never forgot the team's generous gesture of calling her before the pick became public.

The one thing she never missed, even as she warmed to life in Florida, was Jets training camp. Each summer, she took two weeks, headed up the East Coast, and relived the event that had brought her such joy since childhood. On one trip, she stayed with her former coworker, Kathy Reade, and attended a scrimmage the Jets were hosting against the Philadelphia Eagles. Dressed in her usual green and white, Connie sat in the stands and chatted with people about different aspects of the game. One Eagles employee overheard her and complimented Kathy's boss that the Jets had a "stands hostess" for the event. Connie also got to witness part of a young, hospitable Pete Carroll's brief tenure as Jets head coach during training camp in 1994; he generously allowed her son, Chris, to act as unofficial ball boy for the week. When Bill Parcells came later, however, he closed off much of the access she enjoyed on such visits. Had Parcells taken the time to speak with her, they probably would have gotten along well—Parcells was a huge fan of Mike Holovak, Connie's beloved mentor, who'd championed her work within the scouting department. But he never did.

Sometimes, her stepdaughter Lisa, now a striking blonde newscaster, accompanied Connie at camp; on many trips, Connie also brought along Chris. There had been one off-season Connie did miss camp: the year she'd given birth to her and John's first child, a daughter. They'd still been living in the condo when Connie got pregnant; early on, she suffered from placenta previa and was subsequently bedridden. As soon as she was allowed back on her feet, she and John were forced to move, since the complex didn't allow couples with newborns to live in the community. They found and settled in a house, and Connie, after another visit to the doctor, returned home with a clean bill of health—the placenta previa was done, they assured her. She fell asleep, but when she woke up later that same day, she saw there was blood everywhere. She was alone in the house; John had already left for a work trip to North Carolina. The only other person she knew in Florida was the realtor, so Connie called her, and she helped the expectant mother get to the hospital. John's boss, group vice president Al Hendrickson Sr., sent the company plane up to North Carolina to get John. The next thing Connie knew, she was lying in a hospital bed; when she glanced down at the foot of it, there was John's boss—he'd stayed patiently with her the whole time. Connie was moved to another hospital before she finally delivered her little girl. Born premature at 24 weeks, she was 12 inches long and weighed only 1 pound, 12 ounces, measurements that stayed forever etched in the young mother's memory. There wasn't much that could be done at the time for babies born so premature; little Lynne Ann, named after her grandmother Evelyn, lived only five days. The heartbroken parents took a picture of her before she passed. About two years later, in 1983, a son, Chris, was born.

Connie was an active parent. She was PTA president for four years and, at various intervals, the boys' basketball coach, the head softball coach, an assistant coach on the baseball team and the boys' flag football team, and the athletic director for a boys' and also a girls' recreational league. She also coached three girls' basketball teams.

Even with that, her football knowledge remained impeccable. A reporter named Steve Hummer visited the Carberg house in Florida one spring to write a column on her before the draft; a tape of the Senior Bowl was on, and Connie, armed with a legal pad that carried her notes, offered plenty of takes on the needs of the Miami Dolphins—the team of interest to the local market—and some prospects out of Florida schools. "Now," Hummer wrote in the *Sun-Sentinel*, "draft day is a housewive's [sic] hobby."[i]

There was one day John, on a work trip, called the house from a boat where Toyota was hosting several VIPs, including a premiere college football coach at the time, Penn State's Joe Paterno. John, thinking of his football-obsessed wife, asked Paterno if he'd be willing to say hello to her via phone.

Connie happened to be at home when they called.

"Connie, I've got somebody here that wants to talk to you," John told his wife, and put Paterno on.

"Connie, this is Joe Paterno," the coach began.

Connie was convinced John was playing one of his practical jokes.

"Yeah, right," she intoned back.

"No, this really is," the coach insisted.

Connie wasn't convinced.

"OK," she said. "If this is Joe Paterno, tell me who was drafted as the first-round draft pick this past year for the Jets." (The Jets' first pick that year had played at Penn State.)

"Blair Thomas," the coach answered.

"Oh. Well, anyone would know that answer," Connie realized. "OK, let me give you a harder one: who was the player that was not a great practice player that got in the dog house with you a lot, but turned out to be a great player for the Jets?"

"Lance Mehl," Paterno answered.

"Oh," Connie said slowly, wonder creeping into her voice. "This *is* Joe Paterno."

"I never had to prove that I was Joe Paterno before," the coach admitted.

In New York, meanwhile, Mark Gastineau's star had risen to stratospheric heights before eventually crashing down. His celebrity dominated New York—his size, his flowing hair, his huge capacity for fun. One time, he was headed somewhere to eat with a teenage Clay Hampton, the son of equipment manager Bill Hampton, and, as they drove along listening to the radio, they heard the station tout a John Cougar Mellencamp concert playing in the area later that day.

"I didn't know John Cougar was going to be there," Mark exclaimed. "He's my friend. Do you want to go to the concert?"

"Yeah," Clay said. "I'd love to go. Do you have tickets?"

"No, I don't have tickets," Mark answered. "Don't worry about it. We'll get in."

There's no way we're gonna get in, Clay thought.

When they got to the arena, they walked up to the door where they needed to present their tickets. Mark explained who he was, but it was unnecessary—the employees had already recognized him.

"John Cougar, he's a good friend of mine," Mark told them. "I don't have tickets, but I want to surprise him."

It worked like magic. He and Clay were allowed to enter. They started walking through the outer concourse, Mark pausing to size up where the stage was, Clay following him blindly. They made it to another checkpoint, which granted access to the concert floor; Mark again explained who he was and why he was there, and he and Clay were allowed to pass. The concert was already going on, but Mark kept walking toward the stage area, where there was extra security. He repeated his line to the guard. The guard let them through, and Clay found himself on the stage, just off to the side—about 30 feet away, he could see John Cougar in the throes of the concert. The musician looked over, saw Mark, and smiled. At one point during the show, he took off the denim jacket he'd been wearing and threw it at Mark, who caught it. Clay never forgot the experience—for a teenager, it was epic.

Nor was Mark's generosity confined to one incident. When a daughter of Bill and Dottie Hampton got married, Mark, one of the players invited to the wedding, swung by the Hampton house before everyone headed over to the church and noticed the limo waiting to carry the bride was a little dirty on the side. Mark approached the driver.

"This car has got to be immaculate," the defensive end insisted. "This is her wedding day."

He gave the driver money and continued, "Get over there and get this thing cleaned before she comes out here. This is a special day for her. It's got to look great."

It was a side of Mark that his friends needed to remember as his struggle with off-the-field demons became more pronounced and led to his early exit from football. They were hard, hard years, with fading dreams, fractured relationships, and even time in jail. Connie lost touch with him for several years but continued to hope he would find his way. Once again, she chose to have faith he would overcome the odds—this time on a far bigger field of play than a three-hour window on Sundays. Then, one summer, he showed up at Jets training camp. Connie hadn't seen him in ages, but she soon discovered her faith in him was rewarded; Mark's tumultuous lifestyle was beginning to change.

In August 2003, just under two years removed from 9/11, a major blackout hit much of the eastern seaboard.[ii] Connie, in town for her annual visit to Jets training camp, was browsing a record store in Manhattan with Lisa, passing time before they were scheduled to meet up with Mark. Suddenly, all the lights went out. The two women walked outside; other people were pouring out onto the street as stores began emptying of customers. They felt powerless and terrified. Suddenly, as if an apparition, they saw Mark down the street and called out to him.

The tall, broad-shouldered ex-player was trying to weave his way through to them, but people had begun recognizing him—even the doormen were yelling, "Hey, Mark!" as he passed. Mark made sure to acknowledge his fans before finally reaching the two women. They realized the blackout had affected public transportation; thousands of people were literally walking out of Manhattan in the summer heat. Lisa had to get all the way back to Connecticut; Connie was staying on Long Island.

"I'll give you guys a ride home," Mark offered.

The ladies, meanwhile, thought they should call their husbands to let them know they were all right. Since Connie's cell wasn't working, they managed to locate a pay phone (with a line of people waiting to use it) on a corner and scrounged for quarters so they could place a call to John, who was instructed to update Lisa's husband Jeff on their situation.

The next task was finding a restroom for the ladies. It wasn't easy; the line at a nearby drugstore was interminable, and even hotels were locking their doors.

"I'll take you to a place I'm familiar with," Mark suggested.

It turned out to be a police precinct. Between his charity work with a police organization and his arrest history, Mark was fairly familiar with the men in blue; at this location, he knew some of the officers. Connie and Lisa were able to go upstairs at the precinct—in the pitch dark—and use the ladies' room.

Grateful, they got into Mark's car. The scene out the car windows as they drove through Manhattan was surreal—pedestrians had taken to directing traffic. The impromptu road trip, however, became a blast—the trio stopped in New Haven for Mexican food, and Lisa was entertained along the way listening to Connie and Mark. They reached Lisa's house in Mystic, Connecticut, around 10:00 p.m.; Mark then turned around and drove Connie all the way to Long Island. Both women remained forever grateful for what he had done.

In late 2012, Connie received a text from Mark and his wife, JoAnn; the defensive end, happily married, was enjoying a fresh outlook on life thanks to rediscovering his childhood faith in Christ. The Jets, meanwhile, had informed him that they planned to confer the organization's highest honor on him: a spot in its legendary Ring of Honor, meant to commemorate players whose contributions to the franchise were too fundamental to be forgotten. Two years earlier, the Jets had an inaugural class that included Joe Namath, Weeb Ewbank, and Mark's linemate, Joe Klecko. This year, Mark was to be one of the inductees, along with Wesley Walker.

Connie was overjoyed by the news. She began talking back and forth with Mark and his family, including his sister and niece.

"Are you coming up?" Mark asked Connie.

"I'd love to," Connie admitted.

"I want you to be here," Mark said. "You are the one that drafted me. I wouldn't be here without you, so I'd love you to come and be part of my family."

So Connie flew up to New York for the event, scheduled for halftime of the Texans-Jets game in October of 2012. Upstairs in a stadium suite before halftime, it was a big reunion—she saw Frank Ramos, the former public relations director, and, of course, Wesley Walker. He and Connie shared a particularly special bond now—in the late '90s, she'd noticed "floaters" in her right eye and found out she had a detached retina. Eventually, she lost the eye entirely and received a prosthesis, which meant she was without depth perception in that eye. This was hard, as she'd always used her eyes to judge players; she'd even had to relearn how to drive under the new conditions. Mark, meanwhile, had his own set of worries as everyone gathered in the suite; he'd lost his voice from a cold and kept praying he'd be able to get through his speech.

As it came time for the ceremony, the players and their invitees were taken downstairs to the tunnel before walking onto the field. Former Ring of Honor inductees had also gathered there, waiting. Connie looked over, and there was Joe Namath. He came running and gave her a big hug.

At halftime, the new inductees and their guests stepped onto the field. Growing up, Connie had not been allowed to go down to the field with her brothers when they sometimes accompanied her dad to watch warm-ups—as a girl, her presence would have been looked at askance. Now, she stood on the 40-yard line, holding up her phone so as not to miss capturing an instant of Mark's triumph. He made it through his speech; he always talked slowly, which prompted the press later to claim he'd been drinking (he hadn't). Mounted high above them and running around the perimeter of the stadium were select names emblazoned in green letters on a white background—members of the Ring of Honor, with Mark's and Wesley's names now among them. Connie stood snapping photos and wearing a Jets jersey bearing Mark's playing number, 99. At one point, as Mark belted out a rousing "Hallelujah!" she raised her arm exultantly. For the woman who'd given so much of her heart to the organization, the moment was a fleeting taste of heaven on earth.

But long after the lights dimmed that evening and the crowd dispersed, a more lasting tribute to her love for the game remained. In MetLife Stadium on the day of a Jets game, toward the upper deck, a parade of names encircles the stadium: Gerry Philbin, Joe Namath, Don Maynard, and other legends who have worn the green and white. Near the banner bearing Weeb Ewbank's name hangs that of Mark Gastineau—a giant, blazing memorial to one of the greatest defensive linemen to ever play the game. But for those who know Connie's story, its presence is also a silent nod to one of the sport's most extraordinary pioneers—a woman who overcame odds of era and gender to follow her passion; who, while earning the respect of legends, became one herself; who, without bitterness or resentment, espoused the ideal of team over self and never lost the first blush of infatuation with the sport she loved. Without agenda, she ultimately proved what so many after her have sought to establish—that a woman's voice belonged in pro football, and that the game itself would be the better for it.

Photographs

The kids who never wanted to grow up:
Chris, Connie, and Bruce.

A young and smitten Lynne and Calvin.

Hanging with Joe Namath was always cool, no matter the decade (top, Peekskill, 1960s; bottom, early 1970s).

Gerry Philbin enjoys the Nicholas family's noted hospitality.

What would Thanksgiving be without the chance
of a Bake Turner serenade?

Life with the Jets: the Nicholas family poses for a photo, while Lou Holtz gets a taste of the Jets' annual Thanksgiving celebration.

What a sorority's little brother looks like ...

Even better than draft day.

Connie sports the jersey given to her by the team before her move to Florida.

Connie joins Mark Gastineau for his Ring of Honor induction.

Acknowledgments

They are two words rarely said enough, and never regretted when spoken. To those who read and edited, then read and edited again (especially Lori Brown Patrick, Dianna and David Meinecke), encouraged (Chris Carberg, John Carberg, Mark and JoAnn Gastineau), granted interviews for the book (including those named below, from football players to family members to friends and neighbors), and made such interviews possible (especially Jets Senior Director of Media Relations Bruce Speight, who allowed me to shadow Connie at Jets training camp ... twice!): thank you. May all who read this story be as inspired by Connie's life as I have been.

~ *Elisabeth Meinecke*

Special thanks to Joe Namath, Lou Holtz, Mark Gastineau, Al Ward, Charley Winner, Mike Kensil, Chris Nicholas, Bruce Nicholas, Philip Nicholas, Nicole Hambro, Lisa Carberg, Dr. Stephen Nicholas, Joe Collins, Bake Turner, Burgess Owens, Mike Stensrud, Gerry Philbin, Chuck Ramsey, Emerson and Enez Boozer, Wesley Walker, Marty Lyons, Clay Hampton, Frank Ramos, Bruce Harper, Joe Pagliei, Casey Merrill, Dan Sekanovich, Kathy

Reade Pandolfo, Gail Baldwin, Jim Pons, George Hill, Bobby Jackson, Doug Plank, Rob Russell, Clyde Davis, Paul and Betty Albert, Charlotte Sohl, Adam Labenow, Maggie Walsh, Patricia Vorrhies Schneider, Cathy Cathey, Terry Giffen, Bobby Mayo, Stuart Lipkind, Cynthia Schmidlin, Jay Convente, Michelle Lawson, Eileen Matthews, Laurie Webster, Al Hendrickson Sr., Ira Liebarfarb, Barry Krauss, Marv Sunderland, Pauline Holovak, Pepper Burruss, Pete Marasco, Denver Public Library

MORE ABOUT CONNIE

Decades after Connie Nicholas Carberg became the NFL's first female scout, she still has the same passion that made such an impact. Today, Connie wants to share this passion with a new generation of go-getters. Connie has taught football, motivational strategy, and given hope to thousands. Connie wants to ignite passion in every person she encounters, and encourage them to follow their dreams.

For more information on Connie, visit *www.ConnieScouts.com*, or follow her on Twitter (*@conniescouts*). If you would like Connie to come speak at your event or gathering, please email her team at *cc@conniescouts.com*.

Notes

Prologue

[i] The other recognized female NFL scout in league history is Linda Bogdan, the daughter of Buffalo Bills owner Ralph Wilson. Most accounts have her assuming a full-time scouting role for the Bills in the '80s; one article by David Fleming in ESPN Magazine (May 2, 2012) titled "Time to Re-Evaluate" has her taking a part-time scouting role by the late 1970s. An article from *The Sporting News*' Dick Young in 1976 identifies Connie as the first female scout for an NFL franchise; Bogdan, according to Fleming, was the first to do so full time.

Chapter 1

[i] Journalists screaming in press box: Bob Considine, "Bobby Thomson's 9th-Hour Homer Withers Dodgers," St. Petersburg Times, Oct. 4, 1951: 19.

[ii] Draft picks: Associated Press, "Jets Hope to Make Fans Forget Titans," The Milwaukee Sentinel, Sept. 2, 1963.

Playbooks: The Titans started using playbooks in either 1962 or 1963, likely depending on how you define "playbook." William Wallace in *The New York Times* article "Jets Start Drills and Learn Huddle," which ran July 12, 1963, indicates the team went until the 1963 season without them; William J. Ryczek in "Crash of the Titans" (McFarland Books, May 5, 2009) indicates 1962. However, Ryczek writes the playbook in 1962 was "unlike the books used by most teams, loose-leaf notebooks filled with mimeographed copies of preprinted plays." "The Titans' playbook," he continues, "was a small, spiral notebook filled with blank sheets. The players were to copy plays into their books during sessions in which the coaches wrote them on a blackboard."

Players' salaries: figures obtained directly from NFLPA Communications; also, Debra Bell, "U.S. News Questioned Football's Future Nearly 45 Years Ago," U.S. News & World Report, Feb. 1, 2013: online:

http://www.usnews.com/news/blogs/press-past/2013/02/01/us-news-questioned-pro-footballs-future-nearly-45-years-ago

Players working in the offseason to support their families: telephone interview with Jets defensive end Gerry Philbin, who detailed several of the jobs Jets players (drafted in '64 or later) held in their careers, including insurance salesman, printing salesman, and teaching. Two articles verify similar situations in the NFL: "Evolution of the NFL Player," NFL Football Operations (no author) http://operations.nfl.com/the-players/evolution-of-the-nfl-player/; Lubinger, Bill,

---

"Remember When ... Off-season Was Work Time for the Cleveland Browns (and All Pro Athletes)?," The Cleveland Plain-Dealer, May 26, 2010: online.

Chapter 2

[i] History of Babylon: Official Village of Babylon website http://www.villageofbabylonny.gov/history;

Babylon Village Historical Society

http://www.babylonvillagehistoricalsociety.org/aboutus.html;

Town of Babylon official website

http://townofbabylon.com/index.aspx?NID=278 & http://www.townofbabylon.com/index.aspx?NID=230

[ii] This is how the Nicholas family traditionally spelled it.

[iii] Baseball as a morale booster and its relationship with the war: Gerald Balzer and Steven Culbertson: "When FDR Said, 'Play Ball!'" Prologue Magazine (a publication of the National Archives), Spring 2002, Vol. 34, No 1.

The sentiment of baseball drama enlivening households through technology is treated eloquently by Eldon L. Ham in "Broadcasting Baseball: A History of the National Pastime on Radio and Television," where he talks of the "flickering images of television" coming of age in the '50s and the importance of radio to the game. Specific pages of reference include p. 6, 19 and 115.

Wiffle Ball: The Official Wiffle Ball website, http://www.wiffle.com/pages/welcome.asp?page=welcome; also, Chris Epting, "Roadside Baseball: The Location of America's Greatest Landmarks." Santa Monica Press, Second Edition. April 1, 2009; p. 18.

Game began generating interest: Weizel, Richard. "A Nifty Curve Ball, No Windows Broken" The New York Times, Oct. 6, 1996. Online.

Wiffle Ball's marketing: Bill Loving, "Tiny Connecticut Plant Supplies Country's Whiffle Needs," [sic] The Telegraph (Nashua/Southern New Hampshire), April 25, 1987: 11; Eldon Berstein and Fred Carstensen, "Keep It Simple: The Wiffle Ball, Inc.," Business and Economics History Online, Vol. 7 (a publication of the Business History Conference): http://www.thebhc.org/sites/default/files/bernsteinandcarstensen.pdf

[iv] Women's baseball league: Jeneane Lesko,"League History," Official Website of the All-American Girls Professional Baseball League, http://www.aagpbl.org/index.cfm/pages/league/12/league-history

Female jockeys: "Lady Jockeys? Who Needs 'Em?" Life Magazine, Dec. 13, 1968: 33.

List of Associated Press Female Athletes of the Year: Siegel, Alice and Margo McLoone: "The Information Please Girls' Almanac," Mariner Books, 1st Edition, April 29, 1995: p. 219-220.

Basketball: "Timeline," "Trailblazers," Women's Basketball Hall of Fame website, http://www.wbhof.com/Timeline.html; http://www.wbhof.com/Trailblazers.html

Baseball's female scouts, Edith Houghton and Bessie Largent: Paul Vitello, "Edith Houghton, Rare Woman Among Baseball Scouts, Dies at 100," The New York Times, Feb. 16, 2013: D8.

Football: Women had played football to entertain an NFL crowd at halftime during the 1920s; later, in the mid-60s, there was a women's semi-pro league. A woman first competed during a (men's) pro game in 1970. "The History of Women's Football," Orlando Anarchy website, home of Central Florida and Orlando Florida's Women's Tackle Football team http://www.cfanarchy.com/history.htm; "Women's Professional Football Then and Now," United Women's Football League website, http://www.uwfl.net/index.php?option=com_k2&view=item&id=3:womens-professional-football-then-and-now&Itemid=119; Smith, Kevin M. "Pittsburgh Powderkegs: Perry Graduate Played on Women's Pro Football Team," Pittsburgh Post-Gazette, August 31, 1989: 18. Associated Press, "Pro Debut Tough Chore for Mrs. Pat Palinkas," The Palm Beach Post, August 17, 1971: B-5.

[v] Unable to patronize public bars: Guy Butler, "All-American Girls Must Be That," Miami Daily News, March 16, 1950: 2-B.

Chaperones and appearance: Jane Ridgeway, "Girl Players Follow Rules Laid Down for Men, But Only When On the Baseball Field," The Southeast Missourian, April 27, 1950: 5.

More on appearance: Matt Schudel, "Dorothy 'Dottie' Kamenshek Dead; Women's Professional Baseball Player," The Washington Post, May 22, 201; "Lipstick is a must ...": Associated Press, "Carey Scouts For Girls' League; Can Spot Stars by Flick of Wrist," The Milwaukee Journal, March 31, 1948: 6.

[vi] "In a beauty parlor": (no author provided) "Olympic Girls," Life Magazine, July 31, 1964: 46.

"Men may do well enough ...": Phyllis McGinley, "Women Are Wonderful," Life Magazine, Dec. 24, 1956: 74.

Another good source on the battle of feminine vs. sport is Sally Jenkins' "History of Women's Basketball," WNBA.com, http://www.wnba.com/archive/wnba/about_us/jenkins_feature.html.

Chapter 3

[i] Statistic on education for head of household: "100 Years of Consumer Spending, 1960-61," U.S. Bureau of Labor Statistics, p. 28. Online: http://www.bls.gov/opub/uscs/1960-61.pdf

[ii] Forty franchises: William Johnson, "After TV Accepted the Call, Sunday Was Never the Same," Sports Illustrated, Jan. 5, 1970.

[iii] The account of Howard Glenn's death is drawn primarily from three sources: an article about his teammate, Ernie Banks, called "Death in A Locker Room" by Sandy Pawde in the Sarasota Herald-Tribune,

which quotes extensively from Banks' autobiography, "I Hate the Game I Love,"; the AP article from the day after Glenn's death: "Pro Gridder Howard Glenn Dies After Game"; and the AP article announcing the autopsy results on Oct. 11, 1960, "Football Player For New York Pro Team Died of a Broken Neck."

[iv] Without doctors to monitor ... : Ryczek, "Crash of the Titans." Details also confirmed in author interview with Pagliei.

[v] Dave Anderson, "A Jets History Lesson," The New York Times, Nov. 13, 1977: S5.

[vi] *Ibid.*

[vii] Richard Kostelanetz, "'Nick the Knife,' or, The Life of a Football Doctor," The New York Times, Dec. 19, 1971: SM12

[viii] The story of Dr. Cal's first stint on the sidelines of a professional football game is drawn primarily from his July 20, 1986 op-ed in The New York Times entitled, "Views of Sports; The Diagnosis from the Sidelines"; the game story in The New York Times, "Titans Lose Home Opener, 32-10, as Broncos Score 19 Points in Fourth Period," by Howard M. Tuckner, Oct. 1, 1962; as well as two articles in the Denver Post: "Ken Adamson Out for Year" in the Oct. 2, 1962 edition, and the game story from Oct. 1, 1960 by Harry Farrar, "Broncos Top Titans 32-10."

[ix] Albert's resume was reconstructed from two sources: Mary Louise Smith, "Our Heroes: Lebanon Gunner Recalls Missions Over Europe," The Lebanon Daily News, August 31, 2013, and his obituary published by Kreamer Funeral Home.

---

[x] Willie Mays: Hamill, Pete, "Willie Mays, the Say Hey Kid," The New York Times, Feb. 28, 2010: Page 1, Sunday Book Review.
"Willie Mays Biography—Academy of Achievement." Academy of Achievement. 16 April 2010. Web. 11 May 2015.
http://www.achievement.org/autodoc/page/may0bio-1

"Willie Mays—Baseball Hall of Fame." Baseball Hall of Fame. Web. 11 May 2015.
http://baseballhall.org/hof/mays-willie

Chapter 4

[i] Huddle: William N. Wallace, "Jets Start Drills and Learn Huddle," The New York Times, July 12, 1963: pg. 18; "I've seen sicker cows": Hand, Jack. Associated Press Sports Writer. "Ewbank Hopes for New Era With His Jets," Gettysburg Times, April 17, 1963: 4.

[ii] George Usher, "'Broadway Joe' Changes as Seasons Go By," The Bulletin, Aug. 13, 1985: Section D. Another good resource is a Sports Illustrated piece by Robert H. Boyle from July 19, 1965: "Show-Biz Sonny and His Quest for Stars."

[iii] William N. Wallace, "Lack of Stars Disturbs Jets' Owner," The New York Times, July 17, 1964: pg. 21.

[iv] NEA, "Shea Park Gives National Edge on American League," The Nashua Telegraph, April 3, 1964: 10; Shea being second "all purpose facility" constructed for dual football-baseball use: "History of Shea Stadi-

um," Mets.com, 14 May 2015. Web. Lukas, Paul. "Be It Ever So Humble, There's No Place Like Shea," espn.com, Sept. 26, 2008, http://sports.espn.go.com/espn/page2/story?page=lukas/080926

[v] Morris McLemore, "Joe Namath Strikes It Rich, Signing for $400,000 Plus ... ," The Miami News, Jan. 3, 1965: Section C, pg. 1.

[vi] Anecdotes and information about the AFL-NFL draft wars in 1965 are drawn from a multi-page treatment in Life Magazine's Dec. 10, 1965 issue under the title,"1-A in Football Draft." The primary writer was John R. McDermott.

[vii] Usher.

[viii] Peter King, "Nothing Was Guaranteed," Sports Illustrated Monday Morning Quarterback, July 20, 2013. Web. 12 May 2015.

[ix] Wire story (UPI), "Namath Kisses Stewardess on Return to 'Bama," The Washington Post. 7 Feb. 1965: C1.

Chapter 5

[i] Music: The Hot 100, 1966 Archives, Billboard.com, http://www.billboard.com/archive/charts/1966/hot-100 (accessed 9/10/15). Also, see below.

Daylight Saving Time: Daylight Saving Time, U.S. Department of Transportation, http://www.transportation.gov/regulations/daylight-saving-time; Time Zones, National Museum of History, http://americanhistory.si.edu/ontime/synchronizing/zones.html; Jennifer Vernon, "The History of Daylight Savings Time," National Geographic News, http://news.nationalgeographic.com/news/2004/03/0330_040330_daylightsavings.html (accessed 9/13/2015). Also, see below.

One of the most helpful launching points in recreating the aura of the '60s was the website http://www.the60sofficialsite.com/, maintained by Carl Hoffman, a historian and retired member of the U.S. military. The site is full of '60s nostalgia & people reminiscing about the decade, including an entertaining first-hand account on the impact of Daylight Saving Time and the concept of the old and new mix, and competing sounds, in music. "When it comes to the 60's, what I really remember was how great radio was," one commenter named Pamela Drake wrote. "The Fifth Dimension was wonderful. The Supremes were huge—everybody in school danced to them. The Song of the Year 1969 was "Aquarius". Creedence Clearwater Revival was my favorite pop group. "Venus" by Shocking Blue was huge in 1969 too. The Doors were on the charts in 1968. And the top 40 was a complete mix of old and young pop. Frank Sinatra could be in the Top Ten with The Beatles, Smokey Robinson and Astrid Gilberto. It hasn't been like that since. I miss that."

(http://www.the60sofficialsite.com/60s_Memories_From_Our_Visitors.html, accessed 9/10/15).

Another helpful entry was by Clark Richards, "Baby Boomer Music: The Opportunity to Listen to Your Favorite 60s Music Is Just a Click Away,"
(http://www.the60sofficialsite.com/Baby_Boomer_Music_The_
Opportuni-
ty_to_Listen_to_Your_Favorite_60's_Music_is_Just_
a_
Click_Away.html, accessed 9/10/15).

[ii] Pantsuits, shortsuits: "See Through Break Through?," Life Magazine, Oct., 18, 1968: 61; "The Short-Cut Pantsuit," Life Magazine, June 23, 1967: 43; "Pantsuits—Now They've Got It All," Life Magazine, Oct. 7, 1966.
Restaurants debate: *Ibid*, "See Through Break Through": 62.

[iii] To help with ironing and other household chores, Lynne hired a lady named Delia Westbrook; they became so close that Delia named two of her nine children after Lynne and Calvin Nicholas.

Chapter 6

[i] Sauer's views on football are drawn from an obituary by Frank Litsky and Daniel E. Slotnik, "George Sauer, Jets Receiver and Rebel, Is Dead at 69," The New York Times, May 10, 2013; another New York Times' piece, "George Sauer's Love-Hate Connection With Football," by Andy Barall on May 17, 2013; and a mini-feature in an undated New York Times Magazine feature online titled, "The Lives They Lived."

[ii] "Walt Turner Helps Build N.Y. Jets From Nothing," Nashua Telegraph, Oct. 15, 1963. The paper appears to mistakenly identify him as "Walter (Bake) Turner;" the Jets' historical roster, however, has no record of a "Walter Turner" playing wide receiver at any point in team history. Turner's first name was actually Robert, though he was often identified by his nickname, Bake.

[iii] *Ibid.*

Chapter 7

[i] The primary source for the information regarding Walt Michaels' view on Namath and the 1968 team, as well as Namath's response, is an NFL Network documentary, "America's Game: The Super Bowl Champions—The 1968 New York Jets"; the author also verified the general environment through interviews with two former Jets, Gerry Philbin and Bake Turner.

[ii] *Ibid,* NFL Network: "America's Game: The Super Bowl Champions—The 1968 New York Jets."

[iii] The recounting of the AFL championship game, for which no complete game footage is available, has been constructed using several sources in addition to the author's independent interviews: the NFL Network documentary "America's Game: The Super Bowl Champions—The 1968 New York Jets"; New York Times reporter David Anderson's game story, "Jets Win AFL Title By Defeating Raiders, 27-23, Before 62,627 Here," 30 Dec., 1968; Hank Gola's article from the New York Daily News, "Joe Namath, Jets Recall the Day

They Took Fateful Super Step in AFL Championship Game vs. Raiders," 22 January, 2011; and a 2014 article by David Anderson, "New York Area Weather Has a History With the Super Bowl," New York Times, 25 January 2014.

[iv] The description of the field is based on the one Joe Namath gave to NFL Network in the "America's Game: The Super Bowl Champions—The 1968 New York Jets" documentary.

[v] "Joe, I've got...": *Ibid,* NFL Network.

[vi] "Not many quarterbacks," Anderson game story.

[vii] Hank Gola, "John Schmitt, Center on 1969 NY Jets, Literally Had Super Bowl Fever," New York Daily News, 28 January 2014. Web.

[viii] Richard Goldstein. "James Nicholas, 85, Leader in Treating Sports Injuries, Dies," The New York Times, 17 July 2006. Web.

[ix] According to The New York Times, in an article published Jan. 21, 2010, reporters Robin Herman and Marcel St. Cyr were "believed to be the first women ever admitted to a professional locker room" in 1975 at the NHL All-Star game.

Chapter 8

[i] Robert D. McFaddon, "Students Step Up Protests on War," *The New York Times*, May 9, 1970.

[ii] Hickel's letter: Max Frankel, "Hickel, in Note to Nixon, Charges Administration Is Failing Youth; Protests Close Over 80 Colleges." The New York Times, May 7,

1970; "Text of the Hickel Letter," The New York Times, May 7, 1970. "Son of Hickel Joining Strike," The New York Times, May 7, 1970.

[iii] Letters to the Editor, The [Babylon] Beacon, May 21, 1970, p. 16. Dr. Cal, who'd grown up Democrat, had been convinced all Republicans were awful people until he started dating Lynne, who was raised Republican. The doctor soon realized all the negative stories he'd heard about Republicans weren't necessarily true; he eventually became a strong conservative.

[iv] Hayes' quotes are taken from an unidentified speech, likely part of a clip from the BBC documentary, "Woody Hayes, the Football Coach."

[v] Terry Frei, "'77: Denver, the Broncos, and a Coming of Age," Taylor Trade Publishing, April 8, 2013, and excerpted in an article by Mike Klis, "One Final Time on Line," The Denver Post, January 23, 2004.

[vi] Phyllis George, deemed a pioneer for appearing on "NFL Today" at CBS Sports as a female sportscaster, was not hired until 1975, as verified in "Gardner Set for High-Visibility Role," credited to the Dallas Morning News and printed in the Toledo Blade, Dec. 27, 1987; p. B11.

Chapter 9

[i] The Jets ... teaching and coaching: Jim Ingraham, "Ohio State woman grad now parttime Jets Scout," The Lantern, April 7, 1976.

[ii] The exact date of the event is unknown; it occurred between the death of Connie's grandfather dur-

ing her time at Ohio State and 1977, when Namath left for Los Angeles.

[iii] Ingraham.

[iv] Winner's backstory comes from the New York Jets Official Yearbook (exact date unknown).

Chapter 10

[i] Dr. Cal had no idea one could negotiate price when buying cars; he walked in to the dealership and paid whatever the sticker price read. It wasn't until he met Connie's future husband, who worked for Volkswagen Porsche Audi, that he discovered one could haggle price when purchasing a car.

[ii] Both the AFL and NFL had inked tremendous contracts that year, and while it wasn't the first time there'd been TV deals, these new incarnations—spurred by networks competing for rights—meant a significant investment in football's potential. William Johnson, "After TV Accepted the Call, Sunday Was Never the Same," Sports Illustrated, Jan. 5, 1970.

[iii] The anecdote of the kicker tryouts is from an article by Paul Zimmerman in the *New York Post*, "Jets: One Foot at a Time, Please" (date unknown).

Chapter 11

[i] The story of Connie selecting Mike Bartoszek has been recreated using author interviews and the previously cited article by Jim Ingraham in The Lantern.

[ii] Dick Young, "Young Ideas," The Sporting News, Dec. 11, 1976: p. 15.

[iii] Red Smith of The New York Times, "Jets Play Waiting Game Until Namath Decides His Future," Ocala Star-Banner, May 13, 1975: p. 14A; Gerald Eskenazi, "Jets Dismiss Winner 'to Save the Team;' Shipp, Assistant, Named Interim Coach," The New York Times, Nov. 20, 1975; p. 68.

[iv] Eskenazi, *ibid.*

[v] UPI, "Holtz Works Magic, not Miracles," Wilmington Morning Star-News, Aug. 20, 1976: p. 23.

[vi] The retelling of Holtz's departure is constructed from an interview with Connie Nicholas Carberg and an article writtein by Tony Kornheiser, "Desire to Do 'Right Thing' Prompted Holtz Decision," The New York Times, Dec. 10, 1976.

Chapter 13

[i] AP, "Jets Tab Michaels Head Coach," The Morning Record, Jan. 5, 1977: p.12; AP, "Walt Michaels Is Rated Top Choice To Be Coach of Jets," Observer-Reporter (Washington PA), Dec. 14, 1976: p. B5.

[ii] Will Grimsley, AP special correspondent, "Namath Wants to Join Rams," The Victoria Advocate, Jan. 8, 1977: p. 2B.

[iii] Quotes appeared in a Newsday article Dec. 18, 1977.

[iv] Rich Cimini, "The Spirit of '77: Once Upon a Draft, the Jets Got It Right," New York Daily News, April 13, 1977.

[v] Harper's story has been reconstructed from author interviews with Bruce Harper and Connie Nicholas Carberg. The following print sources were also consulted:

Harper making the free agent list: Dave Anderson, "Will the Giants' QB Please Stand Up?" New York Times, Sept. 5, 1977, p. 11.

[vi] The author has relied on interviews to reconstruct the events that led to the birth of the NFL Combine; however, information in this paragraph is attributed to the NFL Operations' "National Scouting Combine," accessed online at http://operations.nfl.com/the-players/getting-into-the-game/national-scouting-combine/ (no author listed).

Chapter 14

[i] There are contradictory accounts of who tasked Connie to find a replacement for Mark Stensrud; in one article, Walt Michaels is named as the person. Perhaps he did, in addition to Hickey; Michaels and Connie were extremely close, and he often consulted her on personnel selections. However, according to Connie (from whose perspective this book is told), it was Hickey who called for the event described here.

[ii] "could be the best ... uniform": UPI, "Talented Iowa State Not About to Relax," The Telegraph Herald (Dubuque, Iowa), Aug. 20, 1978: 29.

[iii] The sixth or seventh round classification reflects Connie's perspective from that time.

[iv] "The bowl could attract ... drafted into the NFL": UPI, "Senior Bowl Has No Trouble Reaching Capacity Attendance," The Albany (Ga.) Herald, Jan. 11, 1979: 1C.

[v] "At some point ... Senior Bowl": Don Pierson, "Demand for Pass Rushers Far Exceeds Supply," Chicago Tribune, Jan. 19, 1996: online.

(http://articles.chicagotribune.com/1996-01-19/sports/9601190142_1_cowboys-and-steelers-senior-bowl-dwight-white)

[vi] The anecdote of Mark's call from the Bills, and subsequent reaction, is reconstructed from two sources: Al Harvin, "Jets' Top Draft Picks Get Their Feet Wet," The New York Times, May 15, 1979; Rob Wiley, "The Daily Oklahoman," May 4, 1979: p. 29.

Chapter 15

[i] Celebrations forbidden: Joel Sherman, "New NFL Rules: One Curbs Celebration After Making Play," UPI, August 25, 1984; Mike Puma, "Gastineau, King of Sack," ESPN.com.

Epilogue

[i] Steve Hummer, "Scout Uses the Numbers to Paint a Draft Picture," Sun-Sentinel, April 24, 1988.

[ii] James Barron, "The Blackout of 2003: The Overview; Power Surge Blacks out Northeast, Hitting Cities in 8 States and Canada; Midday Shutdowns Disrupt Millions," The New York Times, Aug. 15, 2003.